ABRAHAM: FRIEND OF GOD

Abraham
Friend of God

An Ethical Biography of the Founder of the Jewish People

by

AMOS W. MILLER

JONATHAN DAVID PUBLISHERS
MIDDLE VILLAGE, N.Y. 11379

Library of Congress Catalogue Card No. 73-6406
ISBN 0-8246-0156-4

PRINTED IN THE UNITED STATES OF AMERICA

TO THE MEMORY OF
MY BELOVED PARENTS

RABBI JOSEPH MILLER

AND

FRANCES H. MILLER

WHOSE LIVES WERE A FULFILLMENT
OF GOD'S COMMAND TO ABRAHAM:
"AND YOU SHALL BE A BLESSING"

Introduction

The prophet Isaiah calls his people to righteous living by demanding of them, "Look unto the rock whence you were hewn. . . . Look unto Abraham your father" (Isaiah 51:1-2). In truth, throughout the ages, Jews, and indeed all decent human beings influenced by the Jewish Bible, have looked to the life of the Patriarch Abraham for guidance and inspiration.

The curtain rises on the life of Abraham with the Divine command, "Go forth from your native land and from your father's house to the land that I will show you" (Genesis 12:1). His positive response to God's call made Abraham not only the founder of the Jewish faith and father of the Jewish people, but also the spiritual father of all who accept the concept of Ethical Monotheism, of a God who not only created the world but demands ethical and moral living from His human creatures.

The story of Abraham's life is recounted in Chapters 12 through 25 of the Book of Genesis. However, in order to understand the full impact and influence of that life, one must read the Biblical account in conjunction with the penetrating comments and observations of the Sages of Judaism found in the Talmud and Midrash. The ancient Rabbis subjected every verse, every word and indeed every letter of the Bible to the most intense scrutiny in order to extract all of the profound wisdom contained therein. In this volume it is my purpose to present, as it were, an ethical biography of Abraham by amplifying the Biblical narrative with the comments of our Sages which add to our understanding of the life of the first Patriarch, and which have made of his life a constant source of inspiration for subsequent generations.

For an understanding of the unique Rabbinic method of Biblical interpretation known as Midrash, I refer the reader to the introduction to my previous volume "Understanding the Midrash."

An ethical biography, unlike a historical biography, does not concern itself with the facts and dates of history; with whether a particular event did or did not actually occur in the manner recorded. Many of the facts of Abraham's life, including the century in which he lived, are the subject of scholarly dispute. However, it is not the historical facts of his life but rather the lessons Judaism has derived from his life that have been of crucial importance in shaping the spiritual development of the Jewish people and that are of abiding significance to this day.

The great importance attached by Jewish tradition to the account of the life of Father Abraham can be gauged from the fact that incidents from his life have been selected as the Torah Reading for both the first and the second days of Rosh Hashonah, a time when Jews are most in need of, and most receptive to, a spiritually uplifting message.

I have written this book for the interested Jewish layman in an attempt to show the relevance of the Rabbis' statements concerning the life of the first Jew to many of our contemporary issues and problems. My own understanding of the Rabbinic text has been clarified and deepened by lively discussion in the classroom and from the pulpit with the men, women and teenagers of my own synagogue, Congregation Beth Sholom of Long Beach and Lido. I am greatly indebted to them for this, as for many other things. I want to express my thanks also to Mrs. Leni Axelrod, Secretary at Beth Sholom, for cheerfully and efficiently typing the manuscript and helping to prepare it for publication, to Mr. Malcolm Sellinger for being so kind as to check the manuscript for errors and to Mrs. Phyllis Smith for designing the book jacket. Above all, I want to thank my wife for her constant support and encouragement which spurred me to complete the book despite the pressure of many other duties.

For the Biblical text I have generally made use of the 1962 Jewish Publication Society translation of the Torah.

However, on numerous occasions a more literal translation was required for the purpose of the Midrashic comment.

God has conferred upon the Jewish people the distinctive title, "the seed of Abraham My Friend" (Isaiah 41:8). It is my hope that this volume, "Abraham: Friend of God" will provide the general reader with an insight into the towering personality of the founder of our faith and people. Through an understanding of the way the Sages of the Midrash viewed the life of this man who was both Friend of God and Friend of Man we may come to a deeper understanding of our own lives as human beings and as Jews; for as our Sages put it, "Everything that Abraham experienced has also been experienced by his descendants."

CHAPTER 1

The Early Years

Genesis 11:26-32

When Terach had lived seventy years, he begot Abraham, Nachor and Haran.

Abraham's father, Terach, sold idols. Once, upon going away, he left Abraham to sell them in his stead. A man came and wished to buy one. Abraham asked him, "How old are you?" When the man answered that he was sixty years old, Abraham rebuked him, "You should be ashamed, a man of sixty wanting to bow down to an object that is but one day old." The man became embarrassed and left.

Another time, a woman came carrying a plate of flour and said to him, "Take this and offer it to them." Abraham, thereupon took a stick, broke all the idols and placed the stick in the hands of the largest among them. When his father returned, he demanded to know who was responsible. Abraham answered, "Why hide it from you? A woman carrying a plate of flour came and told me to offer it to them. When I did so, each idol insisted that it must eat first and the largest idol got up, took a stick and broke all the others." Hearing this, Terach cried out, "Why do you mock me? Do idols have any knowledge?" Abraham then retorted, "Let your own ears hear your lips speak" (Genesis Rabbah).

Abraham was the first iconoclast, the first smasher of idols. He did not hesitate to challenge the idols worshipped by others as gods. Abraham had the courage of his convictions, and the fact that people all around him worshipped these idols did not deter him from revealing their impotence. Today, as well, people worship idols. They deify the state, wealth, power or pleasure by making these the gods whom they worship above all else. We who are the descendants of the first iconoclast, Abraham, must not hesitate to reject completely the worship of these objects which are meant to serve man and not to be worshipped by him. We must proclaim, "Hear O Israel, the Lord is our God, the Lord is One." We must offer homage to the One God alone and not to the sundry idols of our time that are worshipped by so many as gods.

Haran died in the lifetime of his father Terach.

> When Abraham challenged the divinity of the idols, he was delivered into the hands of Nimrod, the king of Babylonia, who said to him, "I shall cast you into the fire and let the God whom you worship come and save you from it." Haran, the brother of Abraham, was present, undecided as to whom he should side with. Thought he, "If Abraham is victorious, I shall say that I am with Abraham, while if Nimrod is victorious, I shall claim that I am with Nimrod." When Abraham descended into the fiery furnace and was saved, Nimrod demanded of Haran, "Whose side are you on?" and he answered, "I am with Abraham." Whereupon, Nimrod took him and cast him into the fire where his innards were scorched and he died; as it is written, *Haran died in the lifetime of his father Terach* (Genesis Rabbah).

There are many like Haran who are afraid to take a stand between good and evil, right and wrong, until they see which way the wind is blowing. It was to people such as Haran that the prophet Elijah addressed his stinging rebuke, "How long halt ye between two opinions?" (I Kings 18:25). These are the people who, before they will take a stand on any issue, must weigh the balance of power or, at the very least, read the latest Gallup Poll. Even if eventually they are moved to come out on the side of justice and righteousness, their support is of little value, and they can be of very little help in the battle for justice.

Haran did not emerge unharmed from the fiery furnace as did his brother, Abraham, because he did not possess the faith and conviction of his brother and so as soon as "the going got hot" he was consumed by the flames. Only one who is imbued with true faith and conviction can withstand the heat of the furnace and the pressure of a hostile environment.

Before being cast into the fiery furnace, Abraham was given the opportunity to recant his views about the One God and about idols. "Let us worship fire," Nimrod proposed, but Abraham refused (Genesis Rabbah).

Had Abraham simply acceded to the demand of Nimrod that he affirm his belief in pagan deities, he would have been spared the horrible ordeal, but he courageously refused to do so.

"As with Abraham so with his descendants." Jews throughout the ages have submitted to the fires of the auto-da-fé and to all sorts of other horrible deaths when they could have saved their lives by simply affirming belief in the God or gods of their oppressors. It should not be forgotten that until the time of Hitler a Jew could save his life by the simple expedient of embracing Christianity. That the overwhelming majority courageously refused to do so, that they refused to barter their faith and their integrity for their lives, is eloquent testimony that the indomitable spirit of Abraham continued to live in his descendants.

It is a blot on Christian civilization that it has been necessary for men and women either to renounce their beliefs or to pay for their convictions with their lives. When Galileo, for example, challenged the accepted view of the universe, he was forced by the Inquisition to publicly recant on pain of death. Rare, indeed, is the individual who is willing to sacrifice his life for his beliefs. All the more remarkable then is the fact that such a willingness to die a martyr's death characterized not just a handful of courageous Jews, but almost the entire Jewish people.

It was Terach himself who delivered Abraham into the hands of Nimrod (Genesis Rabbah).

One of the most terrifying aspects of the totalitarian state is the willingness of parents to inform on children, and of children to inform on parents. In Nazi Germany, Soviet Russia, and Communist China it is considered not only an obligation, but an honor to spy on the members of one's family and to report to the authorities the slightest deviation from "the party line." Such obliteration of family love and feeling is the natural consequence of the deification of the State. In the name of the State all sorts of monstrous behavior becomes acceptable and even praiseworthy.

And Terach died in Haran.

> Why is this mentioned before the departure of Abraham from Haran when, in reality, Terach did not die until much later? Terach's death is recorded before Abraham's departure, because Abraham had been reluctant to leave his father, thinking, "Shall I leave and bring dishonor upon the Divine Name in that people will say that I abandoned my father in his old age?" Therefore, God reassured him that in these special circumstances it was permissible for him to leave. "Moreover, I will record his death before your departure" (Genesis Rabbah).

Though his father, Terach, was a worshipper of idols, Abraham was concerned about the commandment to honor one's parents. Honor of parents is a cardinal teaching of Judaism, being included among the Ten Commandments. The commandment applies not only to righteous parents but even to parents who are not righteous. The Talmud relates several stories concerning the need to show honor even to parents who seemingly are not deserving of honor.

It is interesting to note Abraham's fear lest, by not showing proper respect to his father, he might cause a *Chillul Hashem,* a desecration of the Name of God. When a Jew does that which is wrong or even that which appears to be

8

wrong, he brings into disrepute his people, his faith and his God. One of the prime commandments of Judaism, therefore, is to avoid any action that might reflect discredit upon our faith. Conversely, we must seek every opportunity to bring about a *Kiddush Hashem,* a sanctification of God's Name, by acting at all times in a manner that will reflect credit upon the Jew and Judaism.

From the fact that Terach's death is referred to at a time when he still had sixty-five years to live, you can learn that the wicked are called dead, even while they are yet alive (Genesis Rabbah).

There are many people who, although they may live to a ripe old age, accomplish nothing worthwhile with their lives. Unfortunately, the epitaph "Dead at 30, buried at 80," applies to the lives of so many. On the other hand, it is also true that "the righteous even after they are dead are considered to be alive." A life nobly lived continues to exert its influence long after the person is buried. His memory serves as a constant source of inspiration to children, family and friends.

CHAPTER 2

God's Call to Abraham

Genesis 12:1

Now the Lord said to Abram: "Get thee out of your country, and from your father's house, to the land that I will show you."

Abraham's first encounter with God may be compared to a man who was travelling from place to place, when he saw a building in flames. "Is it possible that the building lacks a person to look after it?" he wondered. Whereupon the owner of the building looked out and declared, "I am the owner of the building." Similarly, Abraham (seeing the world being destroyed by the flames of vice and wrongdoing) said to himself, "Is it possible that the world has no guide?" Whereupon God called out to him, "I am the Guide, the Master of the entire world" (Genesis Rabbah).

The world often appears to be without a guide, without plan or purpose. But there is a Master of the Universe, who is vitally concerned with the world and its inhabitants. He calls to each one of us as He called to Abraham. The question is whether we heed God's call as did Abraham or whether we ignore it.

God said to Abraham, *"Get thee out."* He used this language instead of simply saying, "Get out," to indicate that "it was for your sake that I created the world." Said God, "Abraham, I looked upon you and created the world" (Tanchuma, Buber).

The entire world was created for the sake of one righteous individual. God realized that in any world he might create there would be many wicked and depraved individuals. But if the world is able to produce an Abraham it cannot be all bad, and its creation is worthwhile. A dedicated teacher should feel that his efforts are well spent if he can have a lasting influence upon one human being. A rabbi, a doctor, a lawyer, often becomes discouraged and wonders if his labors are worthwhile, but if he can affect the life of one human being for good, then all his efforts arc not in vain.

The command to leave his homeland and father's house was one of the ten great trials to which Abraham was subjected. Being compelled to pick oneself up and move is one of the most difficult things for a human being to do (Pirkei d'Rabbi Eliezer 26).

Nevertheless, Abraham withstood the test because he understood that one must be willing to endure hardships and make sacrifices for his beliefs. Time and again, during their long history, Jews have been confronted with the choice of baptism or exile. Although exile meant being uprooted from a land in which they and their forefathers had lived for generations, the overwhelming majority never hesitated to choose exile with all its attendant hardships, and moved on to other lands rather than abandon their faith. The Expulsion of the Jews from Spain in 1492 was only one of a series of such instances.

To what may Abraham our Father be compared? To a phial of myrrh closed with a tight fitting lid and lying in a corner so that its fragrance was not disseminated. But as soon as it was opened and moved about, its fragrance spread. Similarly, God said to Abraham, our Father, "Move yourself from place to place and your name will be made great in the world" (Genesis Rabbah).

Abraham got out into the world and had a profound effect upon mankind. It is not enough to simply live a good life oneself. There are many decent people who have no impact upon the world in which they live. A good person has an obligation to seek to make his influence felt. He has no right to live in his own ivory tower, to live his own insulated and isolated life. Instead, he must move about in society and seek to influence it for good.

There are those who claim that changing one's dwelling place is one of the things that can possibly nullify an evil decree against an individual, for it is written, *Now the Lord said to Abram: "Get thee out from your native land,"* and this is followed immediately by, *"I will make of you a great nation."* However, there are those who disagree and maintain that the case of Abraham was a special case because there it was the merit of *Eretz Yisrael* that benefitted him (Rosh Hashanah 16b).

It was Abraham's change of place which changed his destiny. A change of locale can prove beneficial by enabling a person to climb out of the rut in which he finds himself and to start anew without the disabilities of the past. The statement of our Sages: "He who changes his place changes his luck," has frequently proven true for the individual who needed a fresh start in life, in a new environment, in order to be able to succeed.

In this case, however, there was an additional important consideration in that Abraham was not merely moving from one place to another; he was emigrating to the Land of Israel. *Aliyah,* going up to the Land of Israel to live, is not only a vital necessity if the Jewish state is to survive, but can give an individual an entirely new perspective on life. Settling in the Land of Israel can provide the sense of purpose and direction in life that is often lacking elsewhere, no matter how successful one may be in a material sense.

"To the land that I will show you." Why did God not reveal to Abraham his destination immediately? It was in order to make it more beloved in his eyes and to give him a reward for each and every step. God first places the righteous in doubt and suspense, and only afterwards does He reveal to them His purpose (Genesis Rabbah).

A man of true faith obeys the command of God even if its purpose is not immediately apparent to him, confident that eventually God's purpose will stand revealed. Our own understanding and knowledge is limited and often we cannot understand why God acts as He does but, if we are men and women of faith, we accept God's will, confident that "all that God does, He does for the best." When eventually God's purpose stands revealed, we are more grateful than had it been apparent to us all the time.

God's Promise

12:2-3

"I will make of you a great nation, and I will bless you; I will make your name great, and you shall be a blessing."

Said Abraham to God, "You say '*I will make of you a great nation*' but wherein is this so special? Have You not raised 70 nations from Noah?" God answered, "The nation that I will raise up from you, is the nation of which it is written, 'For what great nation is there, that has a God so close at hand?' (Deut. 4:7)"—(Genesis Rabbah).

There are many nations on the face of the earth but the Jewish nation, despite its numerical insignificance and physical weakness, has always enjoyed a specially close relationship with God. It is this relationship, rather than might or numbers, that distinguishes us from other nations and gives us importance and significance.

God's promise to Abraham to make him a great nation and to make his name great refers to the fact that his coinage became current in the world. And what was imprinted upon Abraham's coinage? An old man and an old woman on one side and a boy and a girl on the other (Genesis Rabbah).

13

The secret of Jewish survival has always been its ability to bridge the generation gap and to enlist the loyalties of young and old. Children are trained from the very earliest to participate together with their elders in the beautiful ceremonies and rituals of Judaism. *And the two of them walked together* (Genesis 22:6), applies not only to Abraham and his son Isaac but to Jewish parents and children in all generations. Moses declared before Pharaoh, "With our young and with our old shall we go" (Exodus 10:9) and so it has ever been.

The threat to Jewish survival today lies in the fact that too often either the old have no understanding or appreciation of the young and thus alienate them from Judaism, or Judaism is made into an entirely child-centered religion with only the child expected to learn and to go to Synagogue, while the older generation remains completely aloof. If Judaism is to survive and flourish we must recapture Abraham's understanding that old and young must be the two sides of the same coin, that there must be an identity of purpose and a common bond between them.

> *"I will make you a great nation"* in that I will give your children the Torah, and because of it they will be called *a great nation* (Numbers Rabbah 11:4).

The greatness of the Jewish people lies in the fact that it has accepted the Torah and lives by it. In numbers and in physical strength we have never been a great nation. Yet, because of the Torah, we have had a greater impact upon mankind than any other people in history. It was Saadiah Gaon who correctly observed, "Our nation is a nation only by virtue of the Torah."

> *"And I will bless you."* God said to Abraham, "I will establish a blessing for you in the *Shemonah Esreh.*" (The first blessing of the *Shemonah Esreh* or 18 Benedictions is called *Avot*—Patriarchs, and ends with the words "the shield of Abraham"; the second blessing is called *Gevurot*, "strengths," referring to God's strength in bringing rain and resurrecting the dead.) Which blessing takes precedence,

God's or Abraham's? Abraham's blessing takes precedence. First we recite "Shield of Abraham" and then we recite "who resurrects the dead" (Genesis Rabbah).

Abraham's blessing takes precedence over God's because God is more concerned about the honor of His people than about His own honor. One cannot love God and hate His people. Our true love of God can be shown only by manifesting love of Israel and of all our fellowmen. Similarly, on the next verse, *"I will bless those who bless you"* the Sages comment that "God is more particular about the honor of a righteous individual than He is about His own honor."

"And you shall be a blessing." Through a play on words, "blessing" (*berachah*) is associated with a "pool of water" (*beraychah*). Just as a pool of water purifies those who are impure so you, Abraham, shall bring near to God those who are afar and shall purify them to their Father in Heaven (Genesis Rabbah).

Abraham was not the world's first righteous man. "Enoch walked with God" but "then he was no more for God took him" (Genesis 5:24). Enoch had been withdrawn from society lest he be corrupted by the evil of the world. "Noah was a righteous man" (*ibid.* 6:9), but Noah was concerned only with his own righteousness. He saved only himself while the world was being destroyed all about him. Abraham was the first righteous individual who conceived his task to be not merely preserving his own righteousness, but affecting for good those who had strayed far from the path of righteousness.

Good people of our day must reject the attitude of Enoch, who withdrew from a corrupt world, and of Noah, who was concerned only with saving himself and his family. They must adopt the attitude of Abraham who believed in the necessity of becoming completely involved in the day to day life of society with all of its failings and vices in order to *be a blessing* and to help purify those who have become impure through wrongdoing.

God's command to Abraham *"and you shall be a blessing"*

has, indeed, been amply fulfilled by the descendants of Abraham. It was Tolstoy who observed that "the Jew is the religious source, spring and fountain out of which all the rest of the peoples have drawn their beliefs and their religions."

Even after the destruction of the Temple and the dispersion of our people, we have continued to bring great benefit to the world and to the people among whom we lived. Jews have aided the economy and made great contributions to science, medicine, literature, music and art. The great Jewish historian, Cecil Roth, wrote a book entitled, *The Jewish Contribution to Civilization*. In the preface to this volume he states, "The outcome of my enquiry has been more than a little surprising even to myself. There is no branch of human culture or civilization which Jews have not touched and enriched. Whether we consider literature or medicine or science or exploration or humanitarianism or art, the Jew has been prominent."

"I will bless those who bless you and curse him that curses you."

These words have been fulfilled throughout history. The principle that the welfare of nations has been directly proportionate to their hospitality to the Jew has worked out in history with almost mathematical exactness. Medieval Spain welcomed the Jew and flourished. She expelled the Jew and decayed almost immediately. England's greatest progress occurred after 1657, the year she readmitted the Jews. Hitler persecuted the Jew and was destroyed, making the name of Germany a curse and a byword among all civilized peoples. America welcomed the Jew and became the most blessed nation on the face of the earth. In the words of Olive Schreiner, "The story of European history during the past centuries teaches one uniform lesson; that the nations which have received and dealt fairly with the Jew have prospered and that the nations that have tortured and oppressed him have written out their own curse."

Notice, also, that the Torah speaks of those who bless the Jew and of those who curse him. The people of the world either bless us or curse us, but they do not ignore us. We have been respected and we have been despised but we have never been disregarded. For good or for bad we have never been ignored, though Jews constitute far less than ½ of 1% of the world's population.

From the fact that God says, *"I will bless those who bless you and curse him that curses you,"* we can see that anyone who is an enemy of Israel is as if he were an enemy of God (Midrash HaGadol, B'haalotecha).

The Catholic and Protestant leaders who are unyielding in their hostility to Israel and to the aspirations of the Jewish people, could well ponder the meaning of this statement. There can be no meaningful dialogue among the faiths, no true rapport and understanding between Christian and Jewish leaders, so long as Christian religious leaders are hostile to the welfare and well-being of the People of Israel and the State of Israel.

"All the families of the earth shall bless themselves by you."

Now this cannot refer to wealth, for they are surely wealthier than we. But it does refer to their asking "of" us. When they get into trouble, they ask of us and we respond to them (Genesis Rabbah).

Jews have always responded to the needs of the country and the community in which they live out of all proportion to their size and their material prosperity. Even when the treatment of the Jew leaves much to be desired, Jews do not hesitate to offer aid and assistance in time of trouble and crisis. In keeping with this tradition, the State of Israel is always among the first to furnish humanitarian aid to countries ravaged by flood and earthquake and has provided technical assistance to underdeveloped nations even when these countries have not demonstrated friendship towards the Jewish State.

Although God's words to Abraham, *"and you shall be a blessing,"* were fulfilled long ago, until recently the rest of

17

the statement, *"all the families of the earth shall bless themselves by you"* had not even begun to be fulfilled. Not only have our great contributions to mankind been ignored and disregarded, but the Jew has been maligned and abused as being a parasite who contributes nothing to society. Perhaps, however, this is beginning to change, and the nations of the world for the first time are beginning to recognize and acknowledge the contributions to human welfare that Jews have been making all along. Recently the Catholic magazine, *The Commonweal*, declared, "Where are the Catholic Salks, Oppenheimers and Einsteins? We still can't point to authorities and discoverers in science equal to those of the Jewish community in America, so much smaller in number than the Catholic community." Also, in 1966 the Nobel Prize was conferred upon two Jewish writers not just because they were great writers, but because they had presented to the world "the cultural heritage of the Jewish people" and because they represent "Israel's message to our time." We can only hope that these are more than isolated instances and represent a trend for the future.

Abraham Heeds God's Call

12:4-6

Abram went forth as the Lord had spoken to him.

Not only did Abraham listen to God's command, though it entailed hardship and inconvenience, but he did so joyfully and not grudgingly. It is of Abraham that the Psalmist speaks when he says, "Happy is the man that feareth the Lord, that delighteth greatly in His commandments" (Ps. 112:1)—(Midrash Tehillim 112).

Performing a mitzvah is not enough. The way one does it, the attitude one displays, is also important. Judaism has developed the concept of *Simchah Shel Mitzvah,* that one

18

should take delight in the opportunity to perform a mitzvah and should derive joy and pleasure from its performance. Outsiders may consider the commandments of Judaism a burden, but one who lives his Judaism knows that the performance of a mitzvah is a source of great joy and pleasure in life.

Abram took his wife Sarai and his brother's son Lot, and all the wealth that they had amassed, and the persons that they had acquired (lit: the souls that they had made) in Haran.

If all the inhabitants of the world got together and attempted to create even one insect, they could not endow it with the breath of life. What then is the meaning of *the souls that they had made?* It refers, however, to the converts they had converted. But still, why refer to them as *the souls that they had made?* From this you can learn, that whoever brings a Gentile near to God and converts him, is as if he had created him (Genesis Rabbah).

Judaism is not a chauvinistic religion based on racial and ethnic considerations. It is not true that Judaism has always been hostile to prospective converts and regards them as being "as hard on Israel as a sore on the skin." From the time of Abraham, Judaism has been concerned with drawing all men away from paganism and substituting a knowledge of the One God for the false gods and false morality of the pagan world. Of course, the fact that Judaism teaches that one does not need to be a Jew to achieve salvation but need only to live by seven basic precepts of morality made it unnecessary to actively seek converts in order to "save souls." The hostile attitude of the Church towards missionary activity by Jews also militated against the seeking of converts.

Today, however, Judaism should and does welcome converts, insisting only that they accept Judaism out of inner conviction and sincerity and not for any ulterior purpose. He who does accept Judaism out of conviction becomes "the son of Abraham, our Father" and experiences a spiritual

19

rebirth, becoming "a new soul" as it were. He is regarded as a Jew in every respect and no distinction is made between him and a born Israelite.

But why does it say *the souls that THEY had made?* It should have said *that HE had made.* The plural is used because while Abraham was converting the men, Sarah was converting the women (Genesis Rabbah).

Sarah was the perfect helpmate for Abraham. She shared his ideals, his values and his goals. Had it been otherwise, it would have been impossible for Abraham to achieve what he did. Although it usually is the man who receives the honor and recognition, behind every successful man there stands a woman who shares his ideals and works quietly but effectively alongside of him.

From the use of the phrase, *the souls that they had made,* we can also learn that whoever teaches his neighbor's child words of Torah, is considered as if he had made him (Sanhedrin 99b).

It is our obligation as Jews to seek to bring other Jews to a realization of what Torah can mean in their lives. Here we have an eloquent testimonial to the role that a teacher can and does play in the life of a child, particularly if the teacher is concerned with the child's moral and spiritual development and not just with the imparting of information. A teacher almost literally "makes" a child in the sense that he molds his character and fashions his outlook upon life. With good reason do our Sages declare that "a teacher is called father and students are called children" (Sifrei, Va'etchanan 34).

And they set out for the land of Canaan. When they arrived in the land of Canaan, Abram passed through the land as far as the site of Shechem, at the terebinth of Moreh. The Canaanites were then in the land.

Why this sudden interpolation of the fact that *the Canaanites were then in the land?* Its purpose is to

20

teach us that even though the Canaanites were in the land, Abraham did not learn from their evil ways (Pesikta Zutrati).

Abraham had the moral fortitude to be able to withstand the pressures towards conformity imposed by any environment. Though surrounded by idolatry and immorality, he remained steadfast in his faith and in his moral character. We, too, are surrounded in our society by all sorts of immorality and false values. However, if we are truly the descendants of Abraham, we should possess something of his moral stamina so that we can resist the pressure to conform to a set of standards and values that we know to be wrong.

His Journeys in the Land

12:7-9

The Lord appeared to Abram and said, "I will give this land to your offspring." And he built an altar there to the Lord who had appeared to him.

Abraham built the altar out of gratitude to God for the good news he had received regarding the Land of Israel (Genesis Rabbah).

We who live in the generation that has witnessed with its own eyes and heard with its own ears the good tidings of the establishment of the State of Israel and the Reunification of Jerusalem in Jewish hands, should we not react as did Abraham? Should we not make of our lives an altar to the Lord and thus express our gratitude to God for having granted us the privilege of witnessing such events and living in such an age?

When Abraham was travelling through Aram Naharaim and Aram Nachor, he saw their inhabitants eating and drinking and acting wantonly. "May my portion not be of this land," he exclaimed. When he arrived at the promontory of Tyre (overlooking the Land of Canaan) and saw the inhabitants weeding their fields when they should be weeded, and hoeing when the fields should be hoed, he exclaimed, "Would that my portion might be in this country!" Said God to him, *"I will give this land to your offspring"* (Genesis Rabbah).

Abraham had no desire to live a life of ease and indolence. He was ready and even eager to do the hard, backbreaking work that building a land required. The pioneers who came to Palestine in the early years of the Zionist Movement knew that backbreaking labor would be required if the land was to be fertile and flourish, and that there were many countries in the world where their lot would be easier. But they welcomed the opportunity to toil and to labor for an ideal.

The State of Israel today stands as a tribute to the toil, sweat and sacrifice of its citizens. American Jewry, also, has understood, and must continue to understand, that prodigious effort and sacrifice on its part are required to insure the continued existence of the Jewish State.

In *all* areas of life, we must realize that nothing truly worthwhile can be attained without effort, and that hard work, particularly for a noble purpose, is truly more satisfying than a life of ease and indolence. "The superstition that all our hours of work are a minus quantity in the happiness of life, and all the hours of idleness are plus ones, is a most ludicrous and pernicious doctrine" (Lord Balfour).

Abraham *pitched his tent (o'ho'lo), with Bethel on the west and Ai on the east.*

Although vocalized as *O'ho'lo* "his tent," the word is actually spelled as *O'ho'la,* "her tent." From this we learn that first Abraham pitched the tent of Sarah and only afterwards did he pitch his own tent (Genesis Rabbah).

Although based on a peculiarity of the text, we have here an indication of the deference paid by Judaism to the woman. Judaism is often accused by those ignorant of its teachings of treating women as little better than property. Nothing, of course, could be further from the truth. In an age when other peoples treated women as little more than beasts of burden, Judaism was most solicitous of the welfare of the woman and treated her with utmost deference and respect. From Abraham's action, we can see that Judaism anticipated the Age of Chivalry by several thousand years.

Then Abraham journeyed by stages toward the Negeb.

He drew a course and journeyed toward the site where the Temple would stand (Genesis Rabbah).

In all of his journeys, Abraham did not lose sight of the ultimate goal of his journey. He always kept in mind that his destination was Mt. Moriah, the site of the Temple.

Like Abraham, we must draw a course and journey towards the site of the Temple. We must keep in mind the ideals, values and goals symbolized by the Temple even though we may be detoured by the exigencies of life from proceeding towards our ultimate destination on a straight line. As long as we keep our sacred goals in mind, we shall ultimately attain them despite all the detours and distractions.

Abraham Journeys to Egypt

12:10-20

There was a famine in the land.

God had promised Abraham, *"I will bless you and I will make your name great,"* yet immediately Abraham was beset by famine. Nevertheless, he did not protest or murmur against God (Genesis Rabbah).

From Abraham, we can learn to accept the will of God without complaint. There is a natural tendency to blame God for all our woes, but a man of faith accepts God's will and remains steadfast in his faith that tomorrow will be a better day.

And Abram went down to Egypt to sojourn there, for the famine was severe in the land.

> What occurred to Abraham occurred also to his descendants. Abraham suffered famine and was forced to go down to Egypt. Similarly, his descendants, because of famine in the days of Joseph, were forced to sojourn in Egypt. God, in effect, said to Abraham, "Go forth and tread out a path for your children" (Genesis Rabbah).

The history of the Jewish people throughout the centuries has in many ways been a re-enactment of the lives of the Patriarchs. That is why the life of Abraham is such a fruitful source of inspiration and guidance for us. Problems that appear today to be unique, and perhaps insoluble, have been faced and dealt with by preceding generations and we can learn from them how we may best be able to surmount our problems and difficulties.

As he was about to enter Egypt, he said to his wife Sarai, "I am well aware that you are a beautiful woman."

> All these years, he was with her and now he says to her, "*I am well aware that you are a beautiful woman*"? Did he not notice her beauty before? What is meant, however, is that although travelling generally affects a person's looks adversely, Sarah retained her beauty (Genesis Rabbah).

Abraham appreciated the beauty of his wife, Sarah. In Judaism, beauty was always something to be appreciated and not denigrated; but beauty was not to be a cause for immorality and unfaithfulness. Sarah's beauty was meant for her husband and not to entice others. Perhaps one of the causes of marital infidelity today is that many a woman is more concerned about "looking pretty" for outsiders than she is in "looking pretty" for her own husband.

Abraham asks Sarah to say that she is his sister so that he might not be killed by the Egyptians. *Pharaoh's courtiers saw her and praised her to Pharaoh and the woman was taken into Pharaoh's palace.*

> It would be better that the wicked be blind because through their eyes they bring evil into the world (Numbers Rabbah 20).

The covetous eye of the wicked, which causes them to seek to take for themselves that which does not belong to them, is the cause of most of the evil and injustice that exist in the world. The last of the Ten Commandments is "Thou shalt not covet." It warns us against casting a covetous eye upon that which belongs to another, whether it be his wife, his house or anything that belongs to him.

And because of her it went well with Abram.

> From this statement the general principle can be derived that "it is always because of the wife that it goes well with a man." A man should always be careful about the honor due his wife because blessing is to be found in a man's home only on account of his wife (Baba Metzia 59a).

Here is but one more indication of the high esteem in which the woman has always been held in the Jewish tradition. Indeed, it is true that a house becomes a home and a source of happiness and blessing for a man only by virtue of his wife who presides over the home. Without a good and devoted wife, a house, no matter how expensive it may be or how lavishly furnished, cannot be a source of happiness and blessing.

But the Lord afflicted Pharaoh and his household with mighty plagues on account of Sarai, the wife of Abram. Pharaoh sent for Abram and said, "What is this you have done to me! Why did you not tell me that she was your wife?"

Pharaoh acts as if he was the one who had been wronged. He had been guilty of terrible immorality but he seeks to cast the blame upon Abraham. How typical of the wicked! Instead of contritely admitting their sins, they cast about for a scapegoat, anybody or anyone they can blame, rather than admit their own responsibility.

CHAPTER 3

Abraham and Lot

13:1-13

From Egypt, Abram went up into the Negeb.

From the use of the term *"went up"* we can learn that the Land of Israel is the summit of the world (Midrash HaGadol).

To this day going to Israel is referred to as *Aliyah,* "going up," and indeed there is nothing more elevating and uplifting spiritually than "going up" to the State of Israel. Throughout the centuries, the Land of Israel has been at the very summit of the hopes and aspirations of the Jewish people. Now that "going up" to the Land is feasible and possible for almost every Jew, *Aliyah* should be given serious consideration by all who desire the "spiritual uplift" that only the Jewish State can impart to one who is proud to be a Jew. If we are not prepared to settle permanently in Israel at the present time, at the very least we should consider it our religious obligation to "go up" to Israel to visit as frequently, and for as long a period, as possible.

Now Abram was very rich in cattle, silver and gold.

From this we learn that Abraham did not lose anything by his move to the Land of Israel (Midrash HaGadol).

There are many who, while interested in *Aliyah,* consider it to be impractical and unfeasible because of the business or professional advantages that would be surrendered and the fear that they will not be able to establish themselves

27

economically in Israel. However, just as Abraham suffered no material loss as a result of his *Aliyah*, while at the same time gaining immeasurably spiritually, so it is with most of those who have the courage to settle in Israel. Business and professional opportunities are available in Israel as anywhere else, and it is possible for most to make the move without undue financial hardship. Whatever loss there may be materially is more than compensated for by the spiritual gain.

Lot, who went with Abram, also had flocks and herds and tents.

What was responsible for all the wealth Lot accumulated? His association with Abraham (Pesikta Rabati 3).

Associating oneself with righteous individuals can be the source of great blessing to a man. "Go forth and see which is the good way to which a man should cleave. Rabbi Joshua said, 'A good companion.' Rabbi Jose said, 'A good neighbor' " (Avot 2:13). The benefits that accrue from such an association can be material as well as spiritual.

Lot benefitted greatly from his association with Abraham. One would, therefore, expect his descendants to deal kindly with the descendants of Abraham. On the contrary, however, not only did they not deal kindly but they repaid us with evil (Genesis Rabbah).

So it has always been in the millennia-long relationship between the Jew and the non-Jew. The Jew has been the source of a great deal of blessing to the world in almost every area of human endeavor. Instead of his contributions to mankind eliciting friendship and gratitude, the reverse has been true all too frequently. The Jew has been repaid with hatred, hostility and persecution.

So that the land could not support them staying together.

If you are surprised at the fact that the land could not support two families, understand that it was not because their possessions were so great but because of the constant quarrelling between the herdsmen (Pesikta Rabbati 3).

It was deficiency in character and not pressure of population or possessions, that made the land too small to contain both groups. Cain and Abel found the entire world too small for just two people to coexist in peace and harmony. The nations of the world today, as in the past, are embroiled in bitter disputes, not because the pressure of population growth makes expansion essential but because they have not learned to conquer human passions and to develop their moral character. The world would be large enough for all nations and all peoples if only we could learn to subdue our animal instincts and to eliminate greed and selfishness.

The animals of Abraham were never permitted to go out unmuzzled so that they would not graze in pasture land that belonged to others. The animals of Lot, on the other hand, were not muzzled because Lot and his shepherds had no qualms about their flock grazing upon land that did not belong to them (Genesis Rabbah).

The quarrel between the shepherds of Abraham and Lot stemmed, in part, from their attitude towards the property of others. Abraham went to great lengths to avoid even the semblance of theft. There are many who while technically heeding the admonition, "Thou shalt not steal," tend to interpret it loosely giving themselves the benefit of the doubt in all questionable circumstances. If theft is wrong, then even a "little" theft is also wrong. We must be careful to scrupulously respect the property rights of others.

When Abraham's shepherds rebuked the shepherds of Lot for their improper use of the property of others, the latter retorted that God had promised the land to Abraham and since Abraham was childless, Lot would ultimately inherit the land anyway, and therefore no theft was involved (Genesis Rabbah).

People frequently go to great lengths to rationalize unethical actions. When one is looking for an excuse or a pretext to do something wrong, he usually can find it. Such rationalizations, however, do not make the action any less immoral, and should be recognized for what they are.

And there was quarreling between the herdsmen of Abram's cattle and those of Lot's cattle—the Canaanite and the Perizitte were then dwelling in the land.

The latter phrase seems both superfluous and out of place. The connection between the two, however, is that "when there is strife between brothers, outsiders become entrenched" (Source Unknown, quoted in Torah Shlemah).

Internal strife and disunity among Jews benefit only the Anti-Semite who is dedicated to the destruction of the Jew. When the Romans were at the gates of Jerusalem, the Jewish defenders of the city were engaged in fighting among themselves. Well did our Sages observe that Jerusalem and the Temple were destroyed because of the causeless hatred that existed among brothers.

Abram said to Lot, "Let there be no strife between you and me, between my herdsmen and yours, for we are brothers."

They were not actually brothers but Abraham refers to him as such, nevertheless, to emphasize their kinship despite the strife that had existed. Abraham was always willing to waive his prerogatives, thus displaying true humility (Tanchuma, Buber).

When individuals vie for leadership and organizations for prestige or power, they sometimes forget that they *are brothers,* all working for the same cause and ideal. Tragically, too many of us are reluctant to waive the prerogatives we feel are due us even though the cause we all hold in common suffers from our strife. Abraham's example should inspire us to subordinate our own personal ambitions and pride to the welfare of our people and our faith, which should take precedence over all personal rivalries and jealousies.

"Is not the whole land before you? Let us separate: If you

30

go north, I will go south; and if you go south, I will go north."

Abraham allowed Lot to choose even though, by right, Abraham was entitled to first choice, because he was so anxious to preserve peace and to avoid giving the pagan peoples reason to gloat over the strife and contention among Jews. Would that Jewish leaders and organizations today would be as eager to avoid the internecine strife that gives joy and comfort only to the enemies of our people.

So Lot chose for himself the whole plain of the Jordan.

Lot chose the fertile plains of the Jordan because he lusted after fertile land that could make him a wealthy man. He chose to ignore the fact that by settling in or near Sodom, he would constantly be in the company of wicked men. It was his greedy eyes that led to his ultimate downfall (Tanchuma, Va'Yeshev 6).

In our desire to amass material possessions, we run the danger of destroying ourselves spiritually and morally by consorting with unsavory, wicked individuals. We may think that we can remain untouched by their influence but, like Lot, will generally find that our association with them drags us down and destroys our souls.

The Promised Land

13:14-18

And the Lord said to Abram, after Lot had parted from him.

From the fact that God spoke to Abraham immediately after Lot had parted from him though he had not spoken to him all the time that Lot was with him, one can see that it was the presence of the wicked Lot that prevented Abraham from hearing the Word of God (Pesikta Rabbati 3).

Intimate association with wicked people can keep even

the righteous from hearing the Word of God. How much more so can such associations make the average human being deaf to the divine voice that seeks to speak to every man.

"I give all the land that you see to you and your offspring forever."

This was because God saw how Abraham loved the commandments. Said the Holy One Blessed be He, "The entire world belongs to Me and I have sold it to Abraham in return for his having kept My commandments" (Tanchuma, Buber, Be'har).

Whatever blessings Israel has obtained and whatever influence we have had upon the world are as a result of our having kept the commandments of God. Without the Torah and its commandments, we would have been nothing more than an insignificant nation of the ancient world that would have soon disappeared from the stage of history.

When the Children of Israel ultimately acquired the Land of Israel it was in fulfillment of this promise that God had made to Abraham: *"I give all the land that you see to you and your offspring forever."* It can be compared to a king who promised a gift to his beloved friend for having accompanied him faithfully, but the friend died. Said the king to the son of his deceased friend, "Though your father has died I shall not retract my promise of a gift. Come and take it." The king in the parable is the "King of Kings" and the beloved friend is Abraham. God has promised His beloved friend Abraham the land as a reward for having faithfully accompanied Him. Said God to Moses, "Though I promised the Patriarchs that I would give them the land and they have died, I do not retract My promise but rather 'The word of of our God endures forever' " (Isaiah 40:8) — (Numbers Rabbah 15).

The Land of Israel is known as the Promised Land because of the fact that it was promised by God to the Children of Israel. It was this promise and the knowledge that

God would not retract the promise made to our forefathers that sustained the Jewish people during 2000 years of exile. Indeed, the events of recent years have once again proven that "the word of our God endures forever." Even the Catholic Church in an historic document approved recently by the Vatican affirmed the religious significance of the link between the Jewish People and the Land of Israel and declared that "Jews have indicated in a thousand ways their attachment to the land promised to their ancestors from the days of Abraham's calling."

"I will make your offspring as the dust of the earth so that if one can count the dust of the earth, then your offspring too can be counted."

Why the comparison to the dust of the earth? Just as the dust of the earth is to be found from one end of the world to the other, so your children will be scattered from one end of the earth to the other. Just as the dust of the earth is blessed only through water, so Israel is blessed only because of the Torah which is compared to water (cf. Isaiah 55:1). And just as dust can wear out even metal vessels but itself endures forever, so Israel will outlast all the pagan nations (Genesis Rabbah).

The People of Israel have indeed been scattered over the face of the earth, yet have continued to exist. We have outlived and outlasted the great and mighty empires that have sought to destroy us. What is the secret of Jewish survival in the face of exile and constant persecution? It is the Torah which has always been our life giving waters, nourishing and sustaining us under the most adverse conditions.

"Up, walk about the land, through its length and its breadth, for I give it to you."

When God gave Abraham the land, He gave it to him as it was, in an unimproved state. But Abraham immediately improved it, as it is written, *and he planted a tamarisk at Beer Sheba* (21:33). Isaac and Jacob also improved the land (Sifrei, Deuteronomy 68).

It is only the Jewish people that have improved the Land of Israel and caused it to flourish. Under the rule of others, Palestine lay barren and forlorn. It was the Jew, and only the Jew, who planted trees and caused the desert to bloom.

God told Abraham to acquire possession of the Land by walking its length and breadth so that his descendants might enter it as legal heirs and not as robbers (Baba Batra 100a).

It may have been necessary for the Children of Israel under Joshua to conquer the Land by force just as it was necessary for the modern State of Israel to establish its existence through military means. But the Jewish title to the Land does not rest upon force of arms but upon legal inheritance. We are in the Land of Israel not as conquerors of that which belongs to others, but as rightful owners who can trace our legal ownership of the land back to the first Jew, Abraham.

And Abram moved his tent, and came to dwell at the terebinths of Mamre which is in Hebron; and he built an altar there to the Lord.

This is one of the three altars built by Abraham: one at Shechem, the place where blessings and curses are given; one at Ai so that his descendants might be saved from the inhabitants of Ai; and one at Hebron where David was crowned king and a covenant was made (Midrash HaGadol).

Like Abraham we build altars and offer prayers for various reasons. Just as Abraham built an altar at Shechem to pray "for a blessing and not for a curse" so do we pray that all may be well with us. As he built an altar at Ai to pray that his descendants might be saved from destruction, so do we pray for the welfare and well-being of our children. Similarly, the altar at Hebron represents our hope and prayer for the establishment of the Kingdom of David, the Messianic era of peace and happiness for Israel and for all mankind. Our prayers are for the well-being of ourselves, our children, our people and of all mankind.

CHAPTER 4

The War of the Kings

14:1-12

At that time four great kings waged war against five other kings.

These four kings allude to the four great powers of the ancient world; Babylon, Greece, Media and Rome. When you see powerful nations fighting each other, you can look for the coming of the Messiah. You can know this from the fact that redemption came to Abraham because the powers fought against each other (Genesis Rabbah).

Indeed, in our time, the redemption of the Jewish people was, at least in part, an outgrowth of wars between powerful nations. The Balfour Declaration, which first promised Palestine to the Jewish people as a National Homeland, was issued during World War I as a direct result of the conflict between the Great Powers. Later, the rivalry between the two great Super-powers, Russia and the United States, undoubtedly made possible the vote of the United Nations General Assembly on November 29, 1947 to establish a Jewish State in part of Palestine, and thus helped bring about the establishment of the State of Israel.

The war of the four kings against the five is the very first war recorded in the Bible. Said God to those kings, "Wicked ones, you inaugurated warfare; you will perish through warfare." As the Psalmist puts it, "The wicked have drawn out the sword and have bent their bow. . . . Their sword shall enter into their own heart and their bows shall be broken" (Psalms 37:14-15). Thus, the four kings were defeated and destroyed by Abraham (Tanchuma, Buber).

Aggressors throughout history have experienced the truth of this observation, to their own sorrow. Too late have they learned that "those who live by the sword shall die by the sword." The fate of the first aggressor nations of history should, but unfortunately does not, serve to deter others who are bent upon aggression.

The four kings took Lot, the son of Abram's brother, and his possessions, and departed; for he had settled in Sodom.

> What was the cause of Lot's capture? *For he had settled in Sodom.* Thus was the verse fulfilled, "The companion of fools shall smart for it" (Prov. 13:20) —(Genesis Rabbah).

When one chooses, for reasons of greed, to live among wicked people, there is every likelihood that disaster will be the result.

Abraham Involves Himself

14:13-16

A fugitive brought the news to Abram the Hebrew (Ha'Ivri).

> He was called *Ha'Ivri* because the whole world was on one side (*Ever*), while he was on the other side (Genesis Rabbah).

Abraham stood alone in his time, being the only one who believed in One God. His descendants have remained *Ivrim*, "Hebrews," in that they have not hesitated to remain firm in their convictions despite the fact that they are an insignificant minority numerically.

When Abram heard that his kinsman had been taken captive, he mustered his retainers.

Thus it is written, "He stoppeth his ears from hearing of blood" (Isaiah 33:15). (Abraham refused to listen to news about the possible shedding of his relative's blood without trying to do something to help him) (Genesis Rabbah).

It is the responsibility of the good person not only to refrain from evil himself but to do all in his power to prevent the triumph of evil. "Thou shalt not stand idly by the blood of thy neighbor," declares the Torah (Leviticus 19:16). We have a solemn obligation to come to the assistance of those who need our help. One of the most shocking aspects of modern society is the apathy and indifference manifested towards those who are in danger. In the overwhelming desire not to "get involved" in somebody else's misfortune, otherwise law-abiding citizens abandon innocent people to their fate, not even taking the trouble to summon the police.

The odds against Abraham were very formidable indeed, yet he defiantly exclaimed, "I will go forth and fall in battle, if need be, for the sanctification of God's Name" (Genesis Rabbah).

Once Abraham realized what duty required of him he did not permit his course of action to be determined by the odds against him. He knew what he had to do and did it, regardless of what the consequences might be for him personally. It is the duty of a human being to sanctify the name of God by acting nobly even though the cost may be great.

What enabled Abraham, with a comparatively small force, to defeat four mighty kings? Abraham fought not with weapons and armor but rather with prayer and supplication (Leviticus Rabbah 28).

"He mustered his retainers" refers to arming them with Torah; that is why they won the battle (Nedarim 32a).

Said Abraham to the Almighty, "Master of the Universe, had Your glory not fought alongside me and aided me, how could one man have prevailed

37

against such an overwhelming force. They fell into my hands only because You helped me" (Tanchuma, Buber).

After the Israeli War of Independence in 1948 and the Six-Day War of June 1967, the question was raised time and again as to what enabled an outnumbered force to win such overwhelming victories. The answers given by Abraham in explaining his victory remain equally valid today. The Israelis were fighting not for territorial aggrandizement, not to destroy another people, but for the highest values of their faith and for life itself. They were able to achieve victory because they entered battle feeling that God was indeed aiding their cause and that the great moral values of the Torah were assisting them in defeating their adversaries.

And went in pursuit as far as Dan.

> What made him stop at Dan? God said to Abraham, "Your descendants are destined to worship idols at this place" (cf. I Kings 12:29). As soon as he heard this, his strength left him (Mechilta, Amalek 2).

The strength of the Jewish people lies in adherence to God and Torah. The mere thought of the future idolatry that would beset his children was enough to weaken the ability of Abraham to fight against his enemies. How much more so are we weakened when we abandon God in the present!

At night, he and his servants deployed against them and defeated them.

> Whoever attacks the People of Israel to do them harm, is destined to fall before them. The four kings fought against Abraham and were defeated by him; Abimelech fell before Isaac; Esau and Laban before Jacob; Pharaoh and Egypt before the Israelites, etc. And Gog and Magog are also destined to fall before Israel in the future (Midrash Tehillim 2).

Gog and Magog exemplify the forces of wickedness and evil that seek to destroy our people and indeed all civilization. Our ability to defeat and outlive our enemies in the past, gives us hope and confidence that we shall continue to defeat and outlive the forces of wickedness that seek to destroy us in the present and in the future.

He brought back all the possessions.

> Hillel the Elder used to say that Abraham gathered up all the possessions of the kings, all the possessions of Sodom and its allies and all the possessions of Lot and returned in peace without anything at all missing (Midrash HaGadol).

From the use of the term "Hillel the Elder used to say" it is evident that he repeated this thought again and again to stress the great lesson it contains. Abraham sanctified God's name in the eyes of the people of his generation by returning to the rightful owners all the property that he had taken in battle, thus proving that he fought only to save Lot, and not for any personal profit. Similarly, we must strive to show that all that we do is not for personal gain or ulterior motive, but for the Sake of Heaven.

After the Battle

14:17-24

When he returned from defeating Chedorlaomer and the kings with him, the king of Sodom came out to meet him in the Valley of Shaveh, which is the Valley of the King.

> It was called the Valley of the King because there the nations of the world said to Abraham, "You are our king, you are our prince, you are our God." But Abraham answered them, "The world does not lack its king and does not lack its God" (Genesis Rabbah .

Grateful nations often seek to confer kingship and even deification upon victorious military leaders. It takes great strength of character for a military leader to spurn the power and the adulation that is his for the taking. Such strength of character was displayed by Gideon. "Then the men of Israel said unto Gideon: 'Rule thou over us, both thou, and thy son, and thy son's son also; for thou hast saved us out of the hand of Midian.' And Gideon said unto them: 'I will not rule over you, neither shall my son rule over you; the Lord shall rule over you'" (Judges 8:22-23). In our own country, George Washington spurned the throne that could perhaps have been his after he defeated the British at Yorktown. Unfortunately, however, these examples have been the exception rather than the rule. More often, military leaders are only too eager to accept absolute power when it is offered to them, and to seize that power when it is not offered. Witness the proliferation of military regimes throughout the world in our own day.

And Melchizedek, king of Salem, brought out bread and wine.

> Salem is Jerusalem. Its king is here called Melchizedek, meaning "the king of righteousness," to indicate that Jerusalem makes those who inhabit it righteous (Genesis Rabbah).

Whoever dwells in Jerusalem is made righteous by the place itself. One cannot dwell in Jerusalem for even a short period of time without being influenced by the aura of sanctity that permeates every inch of the city. Nothing can be more uplifting and have a greater influence upon the way one conducts himself, than the privilege of dwelling even for a short period of time in the Holy City of Jerusalem (on the name, Jerusalem, cf. 22:14).

Melchizedek blessed Abraham saying, *"Blessed be Abram of God Most High, Creator of heaven and earth."*

> Abraham is here associated with the creation of heaven and earth. Said God to him, "Abraham, the

40

heavens and the earth are Mine. However, because you have made My Name known in the world, I confer upon you that which is above and that which is below." Thus it says, *"Blessed be Abram of God Most High, Creator of heaven and earth"* (Numbers Rabbah 14).

It is true that "the earth is the Lord's" (Ps. 24:1) but it is man who must make the greatness of God manifest upon earth. God welcomes man as His partner for without righteous men and women who sanctify the Name of God by their lives and deeds, God's greatness and glory cannot be made known in the world. By making the greatness of God manifest upon earth through our deeds, we acquire for ourselves the blessings of heaven and earth, both spiritual and material blessings, for it is only by so living that life becomes truly worthwhile.

> Abraham is associated with the heavens and the earth; the heavens, in that his children were privileged to inherit the Torah which was given from the heavens; the earth, in that his children were privileged to multiply as the dust of the earth. And all of this was a reward for his uprightness (Midrash Mishlei 19).

The Torah is indeed our link with heaven. It is only when we live by the ideals of Torah that we, who are the descendants of Abraham, are linked with that which is heavenly. Without Torah our lives are nothing more than a physical existence that never rises above the earthly and the mundane.

"And blessed be God Most High who has delivered Your foes into your hand."

> The people of Israel declare before God: "Master of the Universe, see how the pagan nations subjugate us. They have nothing better to do than to devise plans against us." God answers, "Yes, but what do they accomplish? True they enact decrees against you but I annul and destroy them," as it is written,

41

"Blessed be God, Most High who has delivered your foes into your hands" (Tanchuma, Toledot 5).

The enemies of Israel have ever sought our destruction but God frustrates their evil designs against us. As the prophet exclaims to the nations that seek the destruction of Israel, "Take counsel together, and it shall be brought to naught; Speak the word and it shall not stand; for God is with us" (Isaiah 8:10). In the words of the Haggadah that we recite on Passover eve, "In every generation they arise against us to destroy us but the Holy One, Blessed be He, delivers us from their hands."

And Abram gave him a tenth of everything."

> Abraham was the first person to give tithes (Numbers Rabbah 12).

Although others had offered sacrifices to God, Abraham was the first to understand his obligations to institutional religion. He realized the need to properly support the institutions and individuals who make possible the functioning of religion in society. There are many who while loudly proclaiming their devotion to God, sneer at the religious institutions of our time and refuse to support them. Abraham understood the need for religious institutions and therefore willingly supported the priest of his day.

> It was as a reward for giving the tithe to Melchizedek that *the Lord blessed Abraham in all things* (Genesis 24:1) — (Genesis Rabbah).

Although a person should not give charity with the expectation of material reward, the person who gives generously of his means is frequently rewarded manyfold in both a material and a spiritual sense. As the wise Kohelet observed, "Cast thy bread upon the waters, for thou shalt find it after many days" (Eccl. 11:1).

Then the king of Sodom said to Abram, "Give me the persons, and take the possessions for yourself."

> He thought that Abraham was interested in the money (Pesikta Zutrati).

But Abram said to the king of Sodom, "I swear to the Lord, God Most High, Creator of heaven and earth that I will not take so much as a thread or sandal strap."

In so doing, Abraham sanctified the Name of God so that the King of Sodom should not think that Abraham had fought against the Four Kings for monetary gain. Abraham had fought only to save Lot and his possessions, since Lot was his nephew (Midrash Aggadah).

Abraham's motives had been pure from the very beginning but it was important that even the cynical king of Sodom should be made to realize that there are people who are motivated in their actions not by love of money or power but by love of God and fellow man. We indeed perform the additional *mitzvah* of Sanctifying the Name of God when we can make it apparent even to the most cynical that the good deeds we have performed have been done not out of selfish self-interest but out of religious conviction.

But why was it necessary for Abraham to *swear to the Lord?* Because it is necessary for even a righteous person to control his evil inclination through an oath (Sifrei, Va'Etchanan 33).

Every individual, no matter how righteous, possesses an evil inclination in addition to a good inclination, and sometimes the latter needs reinforcement against the blandishments of the former. When one has taken an oath, even if it be within the innermost recesses of his own heart, to perform some noble deed, the oath makes it easier for him not to heed the subtle arguments of the evil inclination to do otherwise. Judah had the courage to offer himself as a prisoner in place of his young brother, Benjamin, because he had made a solemn vow and commitment to his father, Jacob: "I myself will be surety for him; you may hold me responsible" (Genesis 43:9).

New Year's resolutions, for example, are the butt of much humor, but if taken seriously can serve to reinforce our good inclinations and lead us to do good and avoid evil.

As a reward for declaring, *"I will not take so*

43

much as a thread or a sandal strap," Abraham's children were privileged to receive two commandments, the thread of the *tzizis* and the strap of the *tefillin* (Sotah 17a).

The commandments of Judaism are not a burden to be borne but a privilege to be grateful for. The Jew who puts on tefillin and tzizis each morning, is grateful for the privilege and indeed looks upon it as among the rewards for being a descendant of Abraham. Each morning the pious Jew exclaims, "Happy are we! How goodly is our portion, how pleasant our lot, and how beautiful our heritage!" (Siddur).

"Lest you say, 'It is I who made Abram rich.' "

> Abraham refused to *take so much as a thread or a sandal strap* because he reasoned thusly with the king of Sodom; "God has promised me that He would make me rich, for He said to me, *'And I will bless you; I will make your name great and you shall be a blessing'* (12:2). If I take anything that is yours will you not boast, *'It is I who made Abram rich'*?" (Tanchuma).

Abraham did not want to take the slightest chance that his good fortune and success might be wrongly attributed to the King of Sodom, thus detracting from the praise due to God. We must make it apparent to all, at all times, that we consider whatever material blessings we have, whatever good fortune is ours, to be the result of God's goodness to us and not the result of our own genius or the beneficence of others. Thus do we help to sanctify God's Name in the world.

> From Abraham's refusal to take any of the spoil for himself, giving all to the king of Sodom, you can see that he possessed a good eye (a benevolent spirit) (Midrash HaGadol).

In the *Ethics of the Fathers* we are told, "He who possesses these three qualities is among the disciples of Abraham our Father: a good eye, a humble spirit and a lowly

44

soul" (Avot 5:22). One of the hallmarks of a Jew is a spirit of unselfishness and benevolence. A person who cannot look upon God's creatures with a sympathetic eye and a loving heart is not a true disciple of Abraham, father of the Jewish people.

"For me, nothing but what my servants have used up."

Most serious is a theft that has been consumed for then even the completely righteous are unable to return it (Hullin 89a).

There was nothing that Abraham could do about what his servants had already consumed. There are certain actions for which no restitution is possible, for which there is no remedy. Therefore, they are more serious than wrongs that can be righted. That is why our Sages look with such horror upon words of slander, because once uttered they can not be recalled and the damage can not be undone.

CHAPTER 5

Fear Not, Abraham

15:1

*After these things, the word of the Lord came to Abram
in a vision.*

> The word of the Lord came to Abraham after he
> had returned all the possessions of Sodom and Go-
> morrah (Seder Eliyahu Rabbah).

Abraham was worthy of this relationship with God because he had acted in an exemplary manner in his dealings
with his fellow human beings. The individual who neglects
his responsibilities to his fellowman cannot hope to achieve
a close, intimate relationship with God.

*"Fear not, Abram, I am a shield to you; your reward shall
be very great."*

> Of what was Abraham afraid? He was afraid lest
> one of those whom he had slain in battle had been a
> righteous individual (Genesis Rabbah).

Although the war had been unavoidable if he was to save
the life of Lot, Abraham could not rejoice in his victory,
knowing that there might have been innocent men among
those who were slain. The Jew has never been able to rejoice over the downfall of others. The Israeli Chief of Staff,
General Yitzhak Rabin, speaking at the conclusion of the
Six Day War, articulated this traditional Jewish sentiment:
"The terrible price which our enemies paid touched the
hearts of many of our men. It may be that the Jewish people never learned and never accustomed itself to feel the
triumph of conquest and victory and we receive it with
mixed feelings."

Others hold that Abraham was afraid because he thought to himself, "I descended into the fiery furnace (of Nimrod) and was saved; I entered into battle with the Kings and was saved. Perhaps I have already received my reward in this world, and there is nothing for me in the future world." Therefore God said to him, *"Fear not, Abram, I am a shield to you* and all that I have done for you in this world I have done gratuitously, while your reward still awaits you in the future world. There, *your reward shall be very great"* (Genesis Rabbah).

There are some people who accept every good fortune that comes their way, as being theirs by right. They do not question good fortune, only misfortune. Abraham understood that we have no right to take our blessings for granted. We should constantly exclaim with the Patriarch Jacob, "I am unworthy of all the kindness that You have so steadfastly shown your servant" (Genesis 32:11).

Said Abraham to God, "Master of the Universe You made a covenant with Noah that You would not destroy his children. Then I came along and accumulated *Mitzvot* and good deeds more than he, whereupon my covenant superseded his. Perhaps yet another will come along who will accumulate *Mitzvot* and good deeds more than I, and then his covenant will supersede mine." God answered, *"Fear not, Abram, I am a shield to you.* From you I have raised up shields of the righteous; from Noah I did not" (Genesis Rabbah).

The Covenant of God with Abraham and his descendants is an eternal covenant that will never be superseded by another. Other faiths may claim to be the New Israel and to have superseded the descendants of Abraham as the Chosen of God, but their claim is groundless. No new covenant will ever supersede or replace God's covenant with the children of Abraham, the people of Israel.

The words *fear not* are addressed only to a person who truly fears God. Thus, one can see that from the

47

very beginning of his deeds he feared God (Seder Eliyahu Rabbah).

Only one who truly fears God can be without fear of man. The courage and strength of character needed to face the trials and tribulations of our world can come only from a deep and abiding faith in God and His goodness.

> *"Your reward shall be very great."* Because you spurned the reward of mortal man a great reward is in store for you from Me (Tanchuma, Buber).

He who looks to man for his rewards in life denies himself the far greater rewards, spiritual and material, that can come only from God and that are bestowed only upon those who are not consumed with the desire for reward from their fellowman.

> Where in the Torah is the reward due the righteous stated specifically? It is written, *"Your reward shall be very great."* If Abraham who had not been commanded all of the detailed laws of the Torah was told, *"your reward shall be very great,"* how much more so shall it be with one who fulfills the six hundred and thirteen commandments of the Torah (Midrash HaGadol).

We Jews are indeed blessed in that we have been given a Torah with all of its manifold commandments. Keeping the commandments is not only a great responsibility but also a great opportunity to secure the spiritual reward that comes only to those who have fulfilled God's commandments.

An Heir Is Lacking

15:2-3

But Abram said, "O Lord God, what can You give me, seeing that I continue childless."

> What Abraham said to God was, "Master of the Universe, if I am destined to raise children who will

provoke You, better for me that I continue childless"
(Genesis Rabbah). 73 - 221

Children are a yearned-for blessing but nothing can give
a parent more heartbreak and anguish of soul than a child
who goes astray. Many a parent, seeing the way a child has
turned out, has been moved to cry out, "Better had I been
childless."

> Abraham exclaimed before God, "Master of the
> Universe, of what value is all that You have prom-
> ised me seeing that I have no children" (Numbers
> Rabbah 2).

A person strives and struggles in order to be able to
transmit his material possessions and, more importantly,
his spiritual ideals to his children. If his children are alien
to his ideals and all that he represents, then truly he is
bereft of blessing; nothing that he possesses can be of great
meaning and significance to him.

> What made Abraham so certain that he would not
> have children. Said Abraham to the Almighty, "Mas-
> ter of the Universe, I have looked into my horoscope
> and can see by my stars that I will not have a child."
> To which God replied, "Abraham, abandon your hor-
> oscope. Israel is not governed by the stars" (Shabbat
> 156b).
> God said to Abraham, "You are a prophet, not an
> astrologer." In the days of Jeremiah, Israel wanted
> to engage in astrology, but God did not permit them
> to do so. Said He, "Long ago your ancestor Abraham
> wanted to engage in astrology and I did not permit
> him to do so" (Genesis Rabbah).

Abraham was admonished against placing any trust in
astrology. It is foolishness to seek one's fate or destiny in
the planets and stars. People spend fortunes on astrology
which can have no bearing upon their future. The time and
the money could more profitably be spent in constructive
endeavors that can truly influence our lives and the lives of
others for good.

49

"And the one in charge (Ben Meshek) of my household is Eliezer of Damascus."

Who was this Eliezer of Damascus? According to one opinion he is Lot, Abraham's nephew. "His soul," said Abraham, "longs (*Shokeket*) to be my heir and he is called Eliezer of Damascus because for his sake I pursued the kings as far as Damascus and God helped me" (Eliezer, meaning, "my God helped me"). According to another opinion, the meaning of *Ben Meshek* is "the steward of my house." His name really was Eliezer, and he was called Eliezer of Damascus because, said Abraham, "It was through him that I was able to pursue the kings as far as Damascus." The name Eliezer has the numerical value of 318 which is precisely the number of armed men mustered by Abraham (cf. 14:14)—(Genesis Rabbah).

Neither Lot nor Eliezer were fit spiritual heirs for Abraham. Neither could maintain and transmit his revolutionary belief in Ethical Monotheism in the face of a mocking world. Abraham was concerned not about who would inherit his physical possessions, but who would inherit his spiritual treasures.

Our Sages here point out that the name Eliezer which means "My God helped me" has the numerical value of 318 which, in turn, is precisely the number of armed men mustered by Abraham. Abraham's armed might availed him only because God helped him. Conversely, God helped him in battle only after he had mustered his armed men and prepared himself militarily. God helps those who take all measures necessary to help themselves. The State of Israel won its amazing military victories in 1948, 1956 and 1967 with the help of God but, like Abraham of old, Israel must always be prepared militarily to withstand any attempt to destroy her. Then, and only then, can she rely upon the help of God.

Abram said further, "Since You have granted me no offspring, one of my household will be my heir."

It was to Abraham that Kohelet was referring when he declared, "And I hated all my labour wherein I laboured under the sun, seeing that I must leave it unto the man that shall be after me" (Eccl. 2:18)—(Midrash HaGadol).

If the fruits of Abraham's toil were to be handed down to someone who was unworthy and who was unable or unwilling to perpetuate his ideals, then all of his struggles and sacrifices for his new found faith would be rendered meaningless. Only the knowledge that someone will carry on our efforts and our ideals makes our toil meaningful and worthwhile.

God's Promise

15:4-6

The word of the Lord came to him in reply, "That one shall not be your heir; none but your very own issue shall be your heir." He took him outside and said, "Look toward heaven and count the stars, if you are able to count them."

Here God compares the number of the Children of Israel to the stars, while elsewhere (28:14) He compares their number to the dust of the earth. Once He compared them to the stars, why is it necessary to compare them to the dust of the earth? What God was saying to Abraham was, "When your children fulfill My will they will be above all, just as the stars are above the entire world; but, when they do not fulfill My will, just as the dust is underneath and all trample upon it so shall it be with them" (Aggadot B'reishit).

Israel's position in the world is dependent upon its relationship to God. Without God we are nothing; with God we are everything.

Abraham was told by God, *"Count the stars."* Just

as the stars cannot be ruled by any nation, so Israel cannot be destroyed by any nation (Pesikta Zutrati).

The Jewish people are an eternal people. Many nations have persecuted and oppressed us but none have been able, or shall ever be able, to destroy us.

And He added, "So shall your offspring be."

What is meant by *"so shall your offspring be"?* It may be compared to a man who travelled in a desert many days without finding shade or water. Suddenly, he came upon a tree standing by a fountain of water. Seeing how beautiful the tree was and how excellent its fruit and how beautiful its boughs, he sat down and cooled himself in its shade, partook of its fruit and drank of the water. When ready to continue his journey, refreshed and satisfied, he turned to the tree and exclaimed, "Tree, O tree, what blessing can I bestow upon you? That your shade be pleasant? It already is pleasant. That your fruits be luscious? They are luscious. That a fountain of water shall flow beneath your roots? A fountain already flows beneath your roots. What blessing then can I bestow upon you? Only that all the saplings that shall spring from you shall be like you." Similarly, after seeing the way Abraham conducted himself, God said to him, "Abraham, what blessing can I bestow upon you? That you should be perfectly righteous or that your wife should be righteous? You are righteous and Sarah, your wife, is righteous. What blessing then can I bestow upon you? Only that all the children that are destined to issue from you, may be like you." Thus it is written, *And He added, "So shall your offspring be"* (Numbers Rabbah 2).

God's blessing to Abraham is still the most meaningful blessing that one can offer to any worthy individual; that his children may continue in his footsteps and seek to emulate his noble acts and deeds. The blessing is particularly appropriate for a couple that has been blessed with a good

52

life, material possessions and a good name. All that one can wish them is that their children and grandchildren should be like them.

And because he put his trust in the Lord, He reckoned it to his merit.

You find that Abraham inherited both this world and the World to Come only because he put his trust in the Lord (Mechiltah, B'shallach 6).

Like Abraham, the Jew throughout the ages has been able to survive in this world and to merit the life of the World to Come only by virtue of his complete and abiding faith in God. Without faith, the Jew would never have been able to survive.

In the Messianic Age, Israel is destined to sing a song, for it is written, "O sing unto the Lord a new song; for He hath done marvellous things" (Ps. 98:6). Through whose merit will they be privileged to sing this song? Through the merit of Abraham who *put his trust in the Lord*. It was this kind of faith that enabled Israel to inherit the land (Exodus Rabbah 23).

The people of Israel have always been a singing people. It is truly remarkable that throughout our long history of persecution and oppression we have always been able to sing, whether it be at the synagogue service, around the Sabbath table, at any special occasion or even without an occasion. This ability to sing in the midst of suffering stems from our deep and abiding trust in the Lord which we inherited from Father Abraham.

In our day, we have indeed been privileged to *"sing unto the Lord a new song for He hath done marvelous things."* We have witnessed the beginning of the redemption of our People with the establishment of the State of Israel. Certainly this new song of redemption would have been impossible without the complete *trust in the Lord* that we inherited from our Father Abraham. Despite 2000 years of exile, despite persecution and oppression, the Jew continued to trust in the Lord and to believe with a perfect faith in the return to Zion and the restoration of the Land of Israel. It was this faith in God and in God's promise to Israel that made possible the new song of redemption, the rebirth of the Jewish State in our day.

The Covenant Between the Pieces

15:7-12

Then He said to him, "I am the Lord who brought you out from Ur of the Chaldeans to give you this land as a possession." And he said, "O Lord God, how shall I know that I am to possess it?"

Why was Abraham punished in that his children were subjugated to the Egyptians for 210 years? It was because Abraham went too far in questioning the attributes of God, asking, *"How shall I know that I am to possess it?"* (Nedarim 32a).

The slightest faltering in our unwavering faith that the Land of Israel shall remain the possession of the people of Israel can lead to disaster. It was the reluctance of some influential Jews to believe in the possibility of a Jewish State that undoubtedly delayed its establishment. Had Baron Rothschild and Baron Hirsch and other wealthy Jews enthusiastically supported Theodore Herzl at the very beginning of the modern Zionist Movement, the State, no doubt, could have been established in time to save many of the victims of the Holocaust. They, however, regarded Herzl's dream as that of a madman, believing a Jewish State to be an impossibility.

In May, 1948, had David Ben Gurion and other leaders of the Yishuv listened to friend and foe alike who insisted that to proclaim a Jewish State was suicide, had they faltered for a moment in their faith that a Jewish State could be a reality, there would be no Israel today. Now that the State is a reality, the slightest wavering of faith in its ability to survive despite the enemies sworn to its destruction could be disastrous.

There are, however, those who maintain that Abraham was not complaining to God at all, but simply inquiring by what merit he was to be privileged to possess the land (Genesis Rabbah).

From Abraham's question one can see how desperately he yearned for the Land of Israel (Tanchuma).

He answered, "Bring Me a three year old heifer, a three-year old she-goat, a three year old ram, a turtledove and a young bird."

The purpose of Abraham's question had been to ascertain what he might teach his children so that they could atone for any sins they might commit. God's answer, *"Bring Me a three year old heifer,"* etc. informed him that the sacrifices that would be brought in the Temple would serve as an atonement. Abraham, however, persisted, "Master of the Universe, that is all very well for the time when the Temple will still be standing, but what will be with them when the Temple no longer exists?" God replied, "I have already prepared for them the Order of Sacrifices. When they read before Me the Order of Sacrifices as part of their prayers, I will regard it as if they have actually offered the sacrifices before Me and I will forgive them for all their sins" (Megillah 31b).

The purpose of the sacrifices in the Temple was to atone for sins. The important thing, however, was not the actual sacrifice, but the thought behind it, the desire to atone for sin. Therefore, even after the Temple was destroyed, the mere recitation of the Sacrificial Order was sufficient to atone, because it served the same purpose as did the actual animal sacrifice; namely, it expressed a sincere willingness to atone for sin. This, indeed, is the true significance of all our prayers. Through prayer we seek to indicate our sincere desire to atone for past misdeeds and to avoid future ones. It is the thought behind our prayers, the sincerity with which we offer them, which determines their acceptability before God.

> *A three year old heifer.* Actually, what is meant is three heifers. God was alluding to three types of heifer that would be brought in the future; the heifer sacrificed on Yom Kippur, the heifer brought for transgressing unwittingly any of the commandments, and the heifer whose neck is broken (Genesis Rabbah).

The heifer of Yom Kippur symbolizes the need to atone for "sins between man and God." The second heifer indicates the need to atone for sins which we are not even aware that we have committed. The third heifer, the "heifer whose neck was broken," refers to the ceremony conducted by the elders of a city when a person is found murdered near the city (cf. Deut. 21:1-9). Thus it is intended to symbolize the sense of communal guilt that should be felt whenever a crime is committed.

As human beings we should, of course, feel the need to atone for transgressions we are aware of having committed and even the need to atone for transgressions of which we are unaware. In addition, however, we should feel a sense of responsibility for the sins of society as a whole and the need to atone for those sins as well. We have no right to say, "Our hands did not shed this blood" (Deut. 21:7) in regard to any evil or injustice until we can declare with certainty that we have done all in our power to eliminate the root causes of evil and injustice from society.

He brought Him all these and cut them in two, placing each half opposite the other; but he did not cut up the birds.

> The animals enumerated refer to the various empires of the ancient world; Egypt, Babylonia, Greece, etc. while the turtledove and young bird refer to Israel. What God showed Abraham here was the

various empires ruling and then being destroyed (Pirkei d'Rabbi Eliezer 28).

The Jewish people have witnessed the great empires of the world rise to dominance and then disappear from off the face of the earth. *But he did not cut up the birds.* Israel, though seemingly the weakest and smallest of all, has outlived and outlasted all the great and mighty empires that oppressed her.

Birds of prey came down upon the carcasses, and Abram drove them away.

He took a flail and beat them but they were not smitten. Nevertheless, *Abraham drove them away* (*Vayashev*) by means of repentance. (*Vayashev* "drove away" is associated here with *teshuvah* "repentance") (Genesis Rabbah).

The birds of prey represent the nations swooping down on Israel. Abraham tried to beat them off by physical force but failed. He succeeded only when he made use of the weapon of repentance. Only when the Jew turns to God in repentance are his enemies driven off. The Jewish people cannot rely on physical strength alone. Our most effective weapon in frustrating the designs of our enemies is turning to God in sincere repentance for then we are fortified with the knowledge that we are seeking to be on God's side and therefore can hope to triumph over forces of evil.

The Slavery in Store

15:13-14

And He said to Abram, "Know well that your offspring shall be strangers in a land not theirs, and they shall be enslaved and oppressed four hundred years."

Abraham had asked, *"How shall I know that I am to possess it"* and God answered him, *"Know well that your offspring shall be strangers,"* etc. Woe to a man who utters a word from his mouth without knowing how it comes out. He who speaks in the presence of any man takes his life in his hands. How much more so, then, does one who speaks in the presence of God endanger his own life and the life of his children to the end of all generations (Tanchuma, Kedoshim 13).

A man must be very careful in his speech. One never knows the disastrous consequences that may result from careless words. Just as Abraham would have been better off in this instance had he not opened his mouth, so would we, on many an occasion, be well advised to guard the portals of our lips.

> Moses said to God, "I have read the book of Genesis and seen therein the doings of the generation of the flood and how they were punished, and it was a just punishment; and the deeds of the people of Sodom and how they were punished, and it was also a just punishment. But this people, what have they done to be more enslaved than all the preceding generations? Is it because our Father Abraham (showed lack of faith when he) said, '*How shall I know that I am to possess it?*'; and You said to him, '*Know well that your offspring shall be strangers in a land not theirs*'? If that is the reason, then Esau and Ishmael, being also his descendants, should also have been subjugated. Moreover, the generation of Isaac or the generation of Jacob should have been subjugated rather than the people in my generation" (Exodus Rabbah 5).

Why have the people of Israel been singled out for suffering and persecution? Why has our generation been singled out for the greatest catastrophe in all human history—the murder of six million of our brethren? If it is because of our sins—are we any worse than all other people? Most certainly not! We do not know the answer: we cannot explain or understand the Holocaust, but like Abraham and Moses and all those who have gone before us, we must not lose our faith in a good, kind and just God.

58

"God is not man to be capricious or mortal to change His mind" (Numbers 23:19). Yet, God told Abraham that his descendants *shall be enslaved and oppressed four hundred years* while the actual enslavement in Egypt lasted only 210 years. What is meant, however, by the verse, "God is not man to be capricious or mortal to change His mind," is that God does not change his mind when it comes to doing something good. Even if the generation is not deserving, God "is not mortal to change his mind." But when it is evil that God intends to bring, then He does change his mind on occasion. It is only with reference to the good that God has intended that He never changes His mind (Tanchuma, Masei 7).

How much happier the world would be if only Man would seek to emulate God in this regard! When we make a promise to do something that will benefit others, whether the promise is made publicly or only in the innermost recesses of our own heart, we should scrupulously keep the promise we have made and never go back on our word. On the other hand, we need not feel bound to fulfill a threat we have made in a moment of anger. A promise to do evil can and should be retracted any time, without any worry about "keeping one's word" or "losing face" by not carrying out the threat. Many a tragedy could be avoided if only people would learn that there is nothing wrong in changing one's mind when what was originally intended is harmful or detrimental to others.

"But I will pass judgment on the nation they shall serve, and in the end they shall go free with great wealth."

When Abraham heard, *and they shall be enslaved and oppressed,"* etc., he thought to himself, "Is it possible that a nation that enslaves my children shall escape unscathed, without incurring punishment?" Said God to him, *"I will pass judgment on the nation they shall serve"* (Tanchuma, Kedoshim 13).

Throughout our long history, many nations have enslaved and oppressed us but in the end they have not gone unpunished. The Spanish Inquisition and the Expulsion of the Jews from Spain were followed by the rapid decline of Spanish glory; the Holocaust was followed by the total defeat of Nazi Germany. The rulers of Soviet Russia and of the Arab states bent upon the destruction of the Jew, can well ponder the lesson taught by history from the time of the Egyptian Pharaoh to that of the Egyptian rulers of our day.

> *"I will pass judgment."* When God sent Moses to redeem Israel from Egypt, and Pharaoh refused to allow them to leave, God exclaimed, "Pharaoh has acted properly because I said to Abraham, *'I will pass judgment.'* 'I' does not mean Moses or Aaron but only 'I am the Lord thy God' " (Exodus Rabbah 15).

It is God who is the Redeemer of Israel and God alone. As the Haggadah recited at the Passover Seder puts it, "And the Eternal brought us forth from Egypt—not by an angel, and not by a messenger, but by Himself in His glory."

Undoubtedly, this is the reason that Moses' name is scarcely mentioned in the Haggadah; so that we might understand that it was God, not Moses, who is responsible for our Redemption from Egypt. In the redemption that has taken place in our own day as well, it is important for us to understand that over and beyond all else, beyond even the heroism of the brave men and women of Israel, stands the Lord who alone is our Savior and Redeemer.

> *"I will pass judgment on the nation they shall serve."* God promised Abraham that He would pass judgment on all the nations that subjugate his children. And in keeping with this promise God performed many wonders for the children of Abraham. If God did so many wonders for them on the basis of the two word promise, *dan anochi—"I will pass judgment,"* how much more so will he perform great wonders for us to whom He has made so many promises and uttered so many words of consolation (Midrash HaGadol).

Indeed, the wonders that the Almighty has performed on our behalf in our day far exceed anything recorded in the past. To recount the events leading to the establishment of the State of Israel and the wars fought to defend it since its establishment, is to recount the wonders of the Lord.

> *"And in the end they shall go free with great wealth."* God caused Israel to find favor in the sight of the Egyptians so that the Egyptians might lend them things and they might depart well laden. He did so in order that Abraham might not have the excuse to say that God fulfilled against them *"and they shall be enslaved and oppressed four hundred years"* but He did not fulfill for them *"and in the end they shall go free with great wealth"* (Berachot 9b).

Viewing Jewish history, it has often appeared as if only the *Tochechot,* the prophecies of doom and destruction, came to pass, while all the prophecies of redemption and of a glorious future remained unfulfilled. With the establishment of the State of Israel and the Reunification of Jerusalem, we are witness to the fact that the Biblical promises of redemption and glad tidings are also fulfilled.

Abraham's Death Foretold

15:15

"As for you, you shall go to your fathers in peace."

> Great is peace for even the dead are in need of peace (Sifrei, Naso 42).

Even the dead are in need of peace. We often lose sight of this fact when we arrange for the funeral of a loved one. When one considers the dressing up of the dead, the body being placed on exhibition, the wake that has come to be a part of even the Jewish funeral, and the hilarity and even drunkenness that often accompany *Shiva,* we

61

can only wish that people might learn "even the dead are in need of peace." We must seek to restore the quiet dignity and good taste of the traditional Jewish funeral.

> How could God say to Abraham, *"you shall go to your fathers in peace"* when Terach, Abraham's father, was an idolater? God is here informing Abraham that Terach had repented before he died and thus would be with him in the World to Come (Midrash HaGadol).

Terach may have been an idolator all his life but because he repented before his death, he earned a share in the World to Come. In the words of Maimonides, "Even if one transgressed all his life and only repented on the day of his death . . . all his iniquities are pardoned" (Hilchot Teshuva). While it is never too late to turn wholeheartedly to God, one must not delay repentance in the belief that there is yet time. "Rabbi Eliezer declared to his disciples, 'Repent one day before you die.' His disciples protested, 'Does a man know when he will die?' 'That is precisely the point,' he replied. 'Therefore, a man should repent at once for he may die tomorrow. Thus he will spend all his days in a state of penitence' " (Shabbat 53a).

> A good son can save his father from the punishment of Gehennom. Thus, Abraham saved his father (Source Unknown).

In addition to the well-known concept of *Z'chut Avot*, the Merit of the Fathers, Judaism has a tradition of *Z'chut Banim*, the Merit of the Children. The deeds of the child can redeem the life of the parent even after the parent's death. The Talmud declares that "the son endows the father." Just as a tree is judged by its fruit so is the life of the child a reflection upon the parent even after death.

The Mourner's Kaddish, recited by a child for a parent for eleven months after death, undoubtedly has made such a strong impact upon the consciousness of the Jew because of the belief that if the parent has sinned in any way during his lifetime, the Kaddish, which is a sanctification of the Name of God, will be considered true repentance for the deceased and will redeem him from the punishment of Gehennom. A famous Talmudic story tells of a confirmed sinner who, after his death, appeared to Rabbi Akiba in a vision and pleadingly informed him that the only thing that could save him from intolerable punishment would be the recitation of the *Borchu* and Kaddish by his young son who was completely unlearned. Rabbi Akiba then proceeded to teach the child these prayers and when the youngster arose and recited the Kaddish, he saved his father from perdition (cf. Maurice Lamm, *The Jewish Way in Death and Mourning*, pp. 158-161).

"You shall be buried in a good old age."

God informed Abraham that his son, Ishmael, would ultimately change his ways and repent (Genesis Rabbah 38).

How could Abraham enjoy "a good old age" seeing the wickedness of his son, Ishmael? Therefore, say our Sages, Ishmael must have repented. Whether we enjoy *a good old age* or not is dependent, more than anything else, upon the way our children have turned out in life.

The Fourth Generation

15:16

"And they shall return here in the fourth generation for the iniquity of the Amorites will not be fulfilled until then."

God would not punish the Amorites until their sinfulness fully warranted it (Midrash HaGadol).

God, of course, is omniscient and knows the full extent of the future sins of all nations and individuals. Nevertheless, God does not punish for future misconduct but only on the basis of the actions of a nation or individual at the present moment. Certainly, then, we who are not omniscient have no right to assume the future course of action of any individual and to condemn and seek to punish as if anticipated misdeeds are already accomplished fact.

God was patient with the Amorites until their rottenness was complete. Then He judged them at one time for all their sins, thus guaranteeing that they would never rise again. Jews, on the other hand, are punished by God for each sin as they commit it, so that the accumulated punishment will not be so great as to warrant their destruction. This is a manifestation of God's attribute of Mercy in regard to Israel (Midrash HaGadol).

The accumulated guilt of the Amorites was so great as to render complete destruction inevitable. Far better to be called to account for each infraction of the Moral Code as it occurs, so that guilt cannot accumulate. Parents would be well advised to understand that it is truly a manifestation of the Attribute of Mercy to call children to account at the time of each infraction rather than to allow minor indiscretions to multiply and accumulate until the moral character of the individual is completely destroyed. It may seem cruel at the moment to punish for each misdeed and much more merciful to ignore it, but experience teaches that the converse is true.

A Smoking Oven

15:17

When the sun set and it was very dark, there appeared a smoking oven and a flaming torch which passed between those pieces.

God showed Abraham four things; Gehennom (Hell), Foreign Powers subjugating his descendants, the Giving of the Torah, and the Temple. Said God to Abraham, "As long as your descendants busy themselves with the latter two, they will be delivered from the first two. If they abandon the latter two, they will be punished by the first two (Genesis Rabbah).

The welfare and well-being of the Jewish people are dependent upon allegiance to the Torah and to the House of God. As long as we cling to these two mainsprings of Jewish survival, no force will be able to destroy us; not "foreign powers," referring to external oppression, and not the "fires of Hell," referring to the inevitable effects of moral weakness and rottenness.

God put the question to Abraham, "Which do you prefer? That your children descend into Gehennom or that they be subjugated by Foreign Powers? According to one Sage, Abraham chose subjugation to Foreign Powers. According to another, Abraham at first chose Gehennom but God chose for him subjugation to Foreign Powers (Genesis Rabbah).

Very often in life we are confronted with such a choice. One choice would free us from physical and material oppression but at the expense of our soul; the other would save our souls but appear to doom us to a life of deprivation. In *The Devil and Daniel Webster*, the hero was faced with this choice and chose, to his own profound regret, material comfort at the expense of his soul. It takes a morally strong character to be able to choose material deprivation and spiritual salvation over material prosperity and spiritual degradation. But even when we are tempted to choose the latter, the voice of God manifesting itself through our conscience, should compel us to make the proper moral decision.

The Promised Land

15:18-20

On that day the Lord made a covenant with Abram, saying, "To your offspring I give this land from the river of Egypt to the great river, the river Euphrates".

Thus you see that the Land of Israel was given by the Almighty to the People of Israel by means of a solemn covenant (Mechilta d'Rashbi, Shmot 31).

The title of the Jewish people to the Land of Israel is unmistakeably clear. Certainly it is difficult to understand how anyone who claims to accept the Bible as the Word of God can deny the validity of the Jewish claim to the Holy Land. Apparently the reverence for the Bible of many Christian religious leaders is not quite as great as their hatred for the Jew and the latter blinds them to the clear import of the words of the Bible they supposedly regard as the Word of God.

The descendants of Ishmael point to this verse: *"To your offspring I give this land"* and claim that since they too are the offspring of Abraham, they should also have a share in the Land. Geviha Ben Pesisa answered them, however. "Do you bring proof from the Torah? I also will bring proof from the Torah. It is also written in the Torah, *Abraham willed all that he owned to Isaac; but to Abraham's sons by concubines Abraham gave gifts* (Gen. 25: 5-6)." To this the descendants of Ishmael had no answer and they fled (Megillat Taanit 3).

As the saying goes, "Even the devil quotes Scripture." He quotes, however, only that part which serves his own purposes, ignoring all other passages. So it is with some Christian preachers who delight in quoting the Bible and in maintaining that every word of Scripture is the word of God. They quote only those passages that are convenient to them, but those passages that clearly indicate the Jewish people's divine claim to the Land of Israel or the special relationship that exists between God and Israel are conveniently overlooked or ignored.

The Hebrew uses the past tense, the literal meaning of the words being, *"To your offspring have I given this land."* Not *"I will give"* (*Ehtain*) but *"I have given"* (*Na'ta'ti*). This indicates that the word of God is equivalent to action (Genesis Rabbah).

His mere promise is as though it were already done. "Imitatio Dei," seeking to imitate God, is one of the great principles of our religion. It is our obligation to regard our promise as sacred so that others will feel that when we have given our word, that word is as good as done. "A man's yea should be yea, and his nay, nay."

Why is the Euphrates referred to as *the great river* when it is mentioned last among the four rivers referred to in Genesis 2:14? But, as one Sage observes, "If you touch a person smeared with oil, you too will become smeared with oil" and as another puts it, "The servant of a king is like a king" (Shevuot 47b).

The Euphrates is called *the great river* only when it is mentioned in connection with the Land of Israel. Its greatness is derived from its association with something great. This is why every human being should strive to be associated with great men and with great places. It is such association that can lend meaning and greatness to the lives of people who otherwise would be very ordinary and undistinguished.

CHAPTER 6

Sarah and Hagar

16:1-5

Sarai, Abram's wife, had borne him no children.

> The swine grazes with ten of its young, while the sheep does not graze even with one. God had promised to give Abraham all these nations inhabiting Canaan: the Kenites, the Kenizzites, etc. (15:18 ff) ; but so far, *Sarai, Abram's wife, had borne him no children* (Genesis Rabbah).

By all objective criteria God's promise to Abraham seemed impossible of fulfillment, yet Abraham continued to believe that the promise would be kept. Throughout the millennia of exile, the Jew saw all other nations living in their own land, among their own people, while only he was homeless and amidst strangers. Yet he never lost faith in God's promise that he would return to his own land and rebuild Zion.

In life, we often see the wicked surrounded by their adoring family and fawning sycophants while the righteous seem abandoned and alone. Nevertheless, we must never lose faith that ultimately righteousness will be rewarded.

> God had made Sarah barren at first in order that she might rejoice with children later on; as it is written, *He maketh the childless woman to dwell in her house as a joyful mother of children* (Ps. 113:9) —(Pesikta Rabati 43).

Only one who has been deprived of a great blessing can truly appreciate its importance. Most parents take the blessing of parenthood for granted because they were not denied the blessing. Sarah, however, could better appreciate the blessing of motherhood when it finally came because she had been denied it for so long. If we would only pause to consider what life would be like without all of the blessings that we take for granted, we would be more appreciative of what we have and would enjoy life more.

She had an Egyptian maidservant whose name was Hagar.

Hagar was the daughter of Pharaoh. How then did she come to be the maidservant of Sarah? When she saw the way Sarah conducted herself in the house of Pharaoh, she said, "Better to be a maidservant of Sarah than the daughter of Pharaoh" (Sechel Tov).

Hagar was willing to subordinate herself in order to attach herself to great people. To be closely associated with a great person is a rare but valuable privilege and he who has the good fortune to be able to live in close proximity to such an individual should be willing to make great personal sacrifices in order to do so. Pirkei Avot declares, "Be a tail to lions rather than a head to foxes" (4:20); upon which Maimonides comments, "It is better for a person to be a disciple of someone who possesses more knowledge than he, than to be the master of someone who is inferior to him."

And Sarai said to Abram, "See the Lord has kept me from bearing."

Sarah took the blame for childlessness upon herself rather than seeking to blame her husband. She said to Abraham, *"The Lord has kept me from bearing"* (Tanchuma Buber, Vayera, 32).

The secret of the wonderful marital relationship between Abraham and Sarah was that when things went wrong neither sought to blame the other or to find fault with the other. If fault was to be found, each found it within himself. This remains the secret of a happy marriage to this day. Husbands and wives must learn to refrain from blaming each other when things go bad and to look within themselves for the source of the problem.

> She said, "I know the source of my affliction. It is not, as people tell me, for lack of the proper charm or amulet that I am barren. Rather, *the Lord has kept me from bearing*" (Genesis Rabbah).

Sarah refused to resort to all sorts of magic and superstition. She understood that it was God and not magic that was responsible for her condition. To this day supposedly sophisticated men and women resort to all sorts of superstition, magic and astrology to seek to change their lot. Good luck pieces, charms and amulets are not going to change the condition of anybody and it is time that their use was discarded completely. Even the use by many Jews of a *Mezuza* or a Star of David as a good luck piece should be frowned upon. If a Star of David is worn as a sign of identification with the Jewish people that is fine, but it should not be corrupted into a good luck piece that is expected to have the magical power of bringing good fortune.

"Consort with my maid, perhaps I shall be built up through her."

> He who has no child is as though he were dead and demolished. As though demolished, for it says, *"perhaps I shall be built up through her"* and only that which is demolished needs to be built up (Genesis Rabbah).
>
> Whoever has no child is as if his house is demolished (Midrash HaGadol).

It is the blessing of children that makes life worthwhile. Without children a house is not a home and there is a great void in one's life. In the words of the Psalmist, "Lo, children are a heritage of the Lord; the fruit of the womb is a reward. As arrows in the hand of a mighty man, so are the children of one's youth. Happy is the man that hath his quiver full of them" (Ps. 127:3-4).

And he cohabited with Hagar and she conceived.

70

Why were the Matriarchs barren? So that their husbands might derive pleasure from them, for when a woman is with child she is disfigured and lacks grace. Thus the whole ninety years that Sarah did not bear she was like a bride in her canopy (Genesis Rabbah).

Procreation was obviously not regarded as the only justification for sexual intercourse. Sex was not looked upon by our Sages as something dirty at worst and a necessary evil at best, as was the traditional Christian viewpoint. It is perfectly permissible and desirable to derive pleasure from the relationship between husband and wife but Judaism insists that the sexual relationship must be kept within the bounds of marriage.

And when she saw that she had conceived, her mistress was lowered in her esteem. And Sarai said to Abram, "The wrong done me is your fault."

Said Sarah to Abraham, "You have wrongfully denied me words, in that you have heard me being insulted and have remained silent" (Genesis Rabbah).

There is nothing more uncomfortable than being a bystander caught in the midst of a domestic squabble. Even the refuge of silence is frequently not a refuge at all. One, and very likely both, of the disputants will be offended that the third party stood by silently instead of taking up the cudgels in his behalf.

Sarah said to Abraham, "I have a grievance against you." It can be compared to two people who were in prison. As the king passed by, one of the men cried out, "Grant me justice" and the king gave orders to release him. His fellow prisoner said to him, "I have a grievance against you. You should have said, 'Grant *us* justice' and the king would have released both of us but since you said, 'Grant *me* justice' he released you alone and not me." Similarly, Sarah said to Abraham, "If you had said to God, *we* continue childless instead of *'I continue child-*

71

less' (Genesis 15:2), God would have given me a child just as He has given you. However, since you said, *'I continue childless,'* He has given you a child but not me" (Genesis Rabbah).

When a person prays he should pray not for himself alone but for his entire family and indeed for his people and all mankind. Thus the overwhelming majority of our prayers, particularly our prayers of petition to God, are phrased in the plural because we pray not just for ourselves but for all Israel and for mankind.

"The Lord decide between you and me."

> He who invokes the judgment of Heaven against his fellow is himself punished first. Thus Sarah invoked the judgment of Heaven against Abraham and she died before her husband. This, however, is the case only where justice can be obtained in a temporal Court of Law (Baba Kamma 93a).

We should be very careful about invoking God's punishment upon anyone. The notion that God is at our service to punish those who have aroused our displeasure is not only a childish one but indicates that we regard God as little more than an errand boy to do our dirty work for us. Only when there is a complete breakdown of law and order so that justice cannot be hoped for in the courts, do we have a right to invoke the aid of God to bring about the justice that cannot be achieved in any other manner.

> Whoever plunges eagerly into litigation, does not escape from it unscathed. Sarah should have attained the same age as Abraham but because she said, *"The Lord decide between you and me,"* forty-eight years were subtracted from her life (Genesis Rabbah).

One never knows what the result of lawsuits and litigation might be and, therefore, every attempt should be made to resolve matters amicably without resort to the bitterness that invariably accompanies litigation. Many a person's life has indeed been shortened because he was too hasty to run to court, when with a little patience and tolerance the matter could have been solved amicably.

At the Spring

16:6-16

Abram said to Sarai, "Your maid is in your hands. Deal with her as you think right." Then Sarai treated her harshly, and she ran away from her. An angel of the Lord found her by a spring of water in the wilderness, the spring on the road to Shur.

The Hebrew word for "spring" is the same as the Hebrew word for "eye" (*Ayin*). The same word is appropriately used for both because just as a spring when its waters have ceased is of no value, so the eye when it ceases to well up with water is no longer of any value (Sechel Tov).

The Rabbinic comment can be interpreted to refer to the tears of sympathy and compassion that should well up in the eyes of a human being upon witnessing suffering and misery. When the spring of tears has dried up, and tears no longer come to our eyes when we witness human misery, then our eyes have lost their value in that they are not serving the purpose for which they were intended, which is to stir us to compassion for our fellowman. The prophet Jeremiah declares, "Oh that my head were waters, and mine eyes a fountain of tears, that I might weep day and night for the slain of the daughter of my people!" (Jeremiah 8:23).

And said, "Hagar, slave of Sarai, where have you come from, and where are you going?" And she said, "I am running away from my mistress Sarai."

From the fact that when called *"slave of Sarai,"* Hagar herself referred to Sarah as her mistress, the Rabbis derived the saying, "If your neighbor calls you an ass, put a saddle on your back" (Baba Kamma 92b).

It is futile to argue with someone who disparages you in the hope of convincing him otherwise. This is a lesson that

Jewish defense agencies might well learn in their dealing with anti-Semites. Vile anti-Semitic accusations cannot be effectively countered by arguing with the anti-Semite and trying to prove to him logically that he is wrong. Since the accusations are not based upon reason, they cannot be refuted by reason. A great deal of time, effort and money could be put to more profitable use if we came to realize the futility of trying to argue the anti-Semite out of his anti-Semitism.

Both Abraham and the angel had referred to Hagar as the maid or slave of Sarah, and Hagar then refers to herself in the same terms. So goes the proverb, "If one man tells you that you have the ears of a donkey, do not believe him. But if two tell you the same thing, then you better order a halter for yourself" (Genesis Rabbah).

The criticism of one individual may be dismissed as biased and uncalled for, but if you hear the same criticism from a number of people then it behooves you to take the criticism to heart and to look into the matter more closely. Perhaps it is truly as your critics say and the fault does lie in you. You cannot lightly say that the whole world is wrong and you are right. However, if after self-examination you are convinced that your actions are correct and your motives are pure, you should not change to please your critics.

And the angel of the Lord said to her, "Go back to your mistress, and submit to her harsh treatment." And the angel of the Lord said to her, "I will greatly increase your offspring and they shall be too many to count." The angel of the Lord said to her further, "Behold you are with child and shall bear a son; you shall call him Ishmael, for the Lord has paid heed to your suffering. He shall be a wild ass of a man, his hand against everyone, and everyone's hand against him and in defiance of all his kinsmen he shall camp."

God appeared to the children of Ishmael and asked, "Will you accept the Torah?" "What is writ-

74

ten in it?" they asked. God answered, "You shall not steal" (Exodus 20:13) and they retorted, "The very essence of Ishmael our Father is that of a robber as it is said, *'He shall be a wild ass of a man, his hand against everyone'*" (Sifrei, Deuteronomy 3:43).

The Torah runs counter to the very essence of the character of the spiritual descendants of Ishmael and therefore they have felt constrained to reject the Torah and its teachings in every generation. The Torah imposes the type of moral restraints that they are not prepared to accept and therefore they have regarded the Torah and the People of Torah as their natural enemies to be condemned and abused. The People of Israel at Mt. Sinai, on the other hand, were able to accept the Torah and all its restraints willingly and enthusiastically because they had been conditioned from the time of their father Abraham to accept such restraints and to live by such ideals. The Jewish people throughout the ages have been able to revere the Torah and keep its commandments because there has been no basic conflict between the inclinations and character of the people and the teachings of the Torah they had accepted.

Here we are told of Ishmael, *"he shall camp,"* while in Genesis 25:18 we are told concerning him, *"he fell."* Why the difference? As long as Abraham lived, Ishmael *shall camp;* as soon as Abraham died, *he fell.* Before Ishmael stretched out his hand against the Temple *he shall camp;* as soon as he stretched out his hand against the Temple, *he fell* (Genesis Rabbah).

The descendants of Ishmael could flourish and prosper by virtue of living in close proximity to the living descendants of Abraham. The Jews of Israel would like nothing more than to be able to bring the blessings they enjoy to the entire Middle East. Unfortunately, this is not possible so long as the descendants of Ishmael insist on stretching out their hands in an attempt to destroy the Jewish state and all that the Jewish people have accomplished. "As soon as he stretched out his hand against the Temple he fell." Their unwillingness to make peace with Israel has been the cause of the humiliation and defeat suffered by the Arab peoples. If only they would allow the descendants of Abraham to live in peace, they would be able "to camp" in safety and to enjoy all the blessings that Israel is so eager to share with them.

And she called the Lord who spoke to her, "You are El-roi (The God of Seeing)."

"You see the sufferings of the persecuted" (Genesis Rabbah).

God sees the suffering of the persecuted and He saves them from the hands of those who oppress them. This is, in essence, the message of the entire Passover story. The Jew has faith that God will continue to see the plight of the persecuted and oppressed and will deliver them.

CHAPTER 7

The Covenant of Circumcision

17:1-14

When Abram was ninety-nine years old, the Lord appeared to Abram.

Abraham was ninety-nine years old when God commanded him to be circumcised. Why was he not circumcised in his youth when he first recognized the one God? Why was the command delayed until he was an old man? It was to teach a prospective convert that he should not say, "I am too old. It is too late for me to convert." He can learn from Abraham who was circumcised at the age of ninety-nine (Tanchuma).

How often do we hear people say, "I would like to do such and such but I am too old. It's too late for me to change my ways." We can learn from Abraham that when it comes to doing something worthwhile it is never too late. From this Midrash one can also see the positive attitude of Judaism towards converts. God delayed the circumcision of Abraham "so as not to shut the door in the face of proselytes" (Genesis Rabbah) and to encourage them to take the fateful step no matter how late in life.

Why then did not God command Abraham to be circumcised at the time of the "Covenant Between the Pieces" (Genesis 15), since by that time he was already eighty-five years old? It was because God wanted to make a distinction between Ishmael and Isaac. Ishmael was conceived and born while Abraham was still in an uncircumcised state, while Isaac was conceived and born after Abraham's circumcision and thus issued from a holy source (Lekach Tov).

Not only did Isaac issue from a righteous mother while Ishmael did not; even his father was in a state of purity and righteousness that he had not yet attained at the birth of Ishmael. Circumcision here can perhaps be compared to becoming a citizen in the nation of God. Since at the time of his birth his father was not yet circumcised, Ishmael, at best, was a naturalized citizen in the nation of God and a naturalized citizen can easily renounce his citizenship. Isaac, on the other hand, from the very moment of his birth was a citizen of God's nation because his father had been circumcised prior to his birth. As a natural born citizen, his citizenship could never be revoked for any cause or reason.

And said to him, "I am El Shaddai (God Almighty)."

> The Rabbis derive *Shaddai* from the word *dai* meaning "enough." Upon hearing the command that he circumcise himself, Abraham said to God, "Before I was circumcised, people came and joined me in my new faith. Will they still wish to join me after I am circumcised?" God answered, "Abraham it should be enough (*dai*) for you that I am your God and I am your patron" (Genesis Rabbah).

Abraham was concerned that circumcision which entailed a painful operation would deter would-be converts. Indeed, Christianity, in order to facilitate conversion, abolished circumcision and undoubtedly this contributed to its success. The Jewish people has remained a small people because, while welcoming sincere converts, it never sought to make conversion easy by lowering its standards and requirements. Although these requirements have limited our numerical growth, "it is enough for us" that the Lord is our God and our patron. We willingly assume the extra obligations and duties that being the people of God entails.

> God appeared to Abraham and said to him, "If you accept the Covenant of Circumcision upon your-

78

self it is well but if you do not I will say to the world, 'It is enough (*dai*)' and the world will return to being unformed and void." Thus, the Rabbis say, "Were it not for the blood of circumcision, the heavens and the earth would not be able to exist" (Midrash HaGadol).

Circumcision is the sign of man's covenant with God and submission to His will. Without such submission, mankind would soon destroy itself, and the world would be returned to its primeval state. Of course, the importance of the ritual of circumcision to the survival of the *Jew* can hardly be overestimated. Even Spinoza was moved to declare, "Such great importance do I attach to the sign of the covenant that I am persuaded that it is sufficient by itself to preserve the Nation forever."

"Walk before Me and be wholehearted."

Concerning Noah it is written *Noah walked with God* (Gen. 6:9), while concerning Abraham it is written, *"Walk before Me."* Reading this, one would think that Noah was greater than Abraham because he walked *with* God while Abraham only walked *before* God. But it is not so. It may be compared to a king who had two sons, one an adult and the other a child. To the child he said, "Walk with me" so that the child might not fall, but to the adult he said, "Walk before me." Similarly, to Abraham, whose moral strength was great, God said, *"Walk before Me";* but of Noah, whose moral strength was not great, the Torah says, *Noah walked with God* so that he might not sink into the mud of the generation of the Flood (Genesis Rabbah, Noah 30).

Abraham possessed the moral character to stand upon his own two feet. There was no fear that he might be dragged down by the corrupt environment in which he found himself. Noah, on the other hand, had to be continually watched and encouraged lest he become like all the others. It is the mark of a descendant of Abraham that he is able to swim against the tide, to stand up proudly for what he believes and, even though he be in the minority, not be corrupted by the pressures of the environment. The pressure to conform to the ways of the majority and to be like everybody else is great but a true descendant of Abraham knows how to resist that pressure.

> *"Walk before Me."* Rabbi Yochanan maintains that it can be compared to a flock of sheep walking before the shepherd while Resh Lakish maintains that it can be compared to elders preceding a prince as his escort and making known his coming. According to the view of Rabbi Yochanan, we need God just as the sheep need the shepherd. According to the view of Resh Lakish, God needs us just as the prince needs his escort to make known his presence (Genesis Rabbah, Noah 30).

Both are right. We need God and God needs us. Without God we are lost; but without us, God has nobody to make known His glory in the world. It was through the noble life of Abraham that people first began to appreciate the greatness of the One God. Similarly, it is the task of his descendants to spread the knowledge of God among men. It is only through the way we live and the good deeds we perform that the greatness and glory of God can be made known to all. In this very real sense God needs us. *Kiddush Hashem,* Sanctifying the Name of God through noble actions, is thus one of the great obligations of the descendants of Abraham.

> *"And be wholehearted."* God refers to Abraham as *wholehearted* thus indicating the great importance of circumcision. Despite all the commandments that Abraham had fulfilled he was not called *wholehearted* except with reference to circumcision (Mechilta, Yitro).

There are many important commandments that a Jew is expected to fulfill but if he neglects to fulfill them he remains a Jew, nevertheless. Not so, however, with the ritual of circumcision. A father who neglects to have his child circumcised is in effect declaring that he does not want him to be a member of the Jewish faith and people. "Circumcision is an institution, not a mere ceremony. The son who, on principle, remains uncircumcised will hardly, on principle, remain in Judaism (Leopold Zunz).

"I will establish My covenant between Me and You."

When God said to Abraham, *"Walk before Me and be wholehearted,"* Abraham was seized with trembling. He thought, "Perhaps there is something shameful in me, that I have not been wholehearted until now." But when God added, *"I will establish My covenant between Me and You,"* his mind was set at ease (Nedarim 32a).

Abraham was seized with trembling when he suspected that there might be some imperfection in him, and his mind was not appeased until God assured him that the imperfection was not in himself but in the lack of a formal covenant between him and the Almighty. The righteous man never feels secure in his righteousness. He is always on guard against some shortcoming in himself and strives to improve himself. It is this sensitivity to any imperfection that makes him truly righteous.

From the experience of Abraham one can learn that if an individual seeks to perfect himself, good fortune will be his. For it is written, *"Walk before Me and be wholehearted* (perfect)" and then, *"You shall be the father of a multitude of nations"* (Nedarim 32a).

God demands of us that we constantly seek to perfect ourselves and promises that if we do so, good fortune will be ours. The person who tries to improve himself morally and spiritually at all times will indeed be, like Abraham, *the father of a multitude of nations* in the sense that he will have a lasting influence upon his descendants.

"You shall no longer be called Abram, but your name shall be Abraham."

A change of name is one of the things that can an-

81

nul evil decrees. Abram could not have a child but Abraham could, Sarai could not bear a child but Sarah could (Kohelet Rabbah 5).

A change of name can be either good or bad depending upon the purpose. When the purpose is to run away from one's identity then it is to be condemned. When, as here, it connotes consecration to God and to God's commandments it is not only commendable, but in itself can further the process of consecration. A change of name can signify a desire to make a fresh start in life, free of the debasing influences of the past. In this sense, a change of name can indeed "annul evil decrees" by emancipating an individual from the demoralizing influences of the past. Jews who settled in the Land of Israel and changed their names from those associated with the Diaspora to Hebrew and Israeli names were in effect announcing that in the Land of Israel they were beginning life anew, free from the degrading influences of the Diaspora.

"For I make you the father of a multitude of nations."

Can a convert upon bringing the First Fruits to the Temple make the accompanying declaration (Deut. 26)? There are those who say he cannot because he is unable to declare, *"the land which the Lord swore to our fathers to give us"* (Deut. 26:3). Rabbi Judah, however, maintains that a convert may indeed recite this declaration because Abraham was told, *"For I make you the father of a multitude of nations.* Originally you were the father of Aram From now on you are the father of all the nations." And the law is with Rabbi Judah (Yerushalmi, Bikkurim 1:4).

Abraham is the father of all nations in a spiritual sense. He is the father of all those who sincerely accept the one God and His commandments. One who is born a non-Jew but sincerely converts to Judaism can in good conscience speak of "Abraham our Father." Judaism makes no distinction between the born Jew and the sincere convert. In a spiritual sense the latter is as much the descendant of Abraham, Isaac and Jacob as is the former. There is nothing racial about Jewishness.

"I will maintain My covenant between Me and You, and your offspring to come as an everlasting covenant throughout the ages, to be God to you and to your offspring to come."

One who does not engage in procreation causes the Divine Spirit to depart from Israel. The Torah says, *"to be God to you and to your offspring to come."* Where there exist *offspring to come* the Divine Presence rests upon them but where there is no *offspring to come,* upon whom should the DivinePresence rest? Upon the trees and stones? (Yevamot 64a).

We Jews are a very small people made even smaller by the murder of six million of our brethren by the Nazis. This imposes a great responsibility upon us to see to it that the Jewish people reproduces itself. A declining birthrate may be desirable for some nations but for the Jewish people, both inside of Israel and outside, it could have disastrous consequences. Without Jews there can be no Judaism. Therefore, anyone interested in the preservation of Judaism must be willing to fulfill his responsibility to bring Jewish children into the world.

The literal meaning of the Torah text is *your offspring after you* and the comment of the Sages literally translated means, "When your children come *after you,* i.e., when they follow in your footsteps, the Divine Presence rests upon you; when your children do not come after you, when they do not follow in your footsteps, among whom can the Divine Presence rest." The greatest blessing that parents can have is to have their children follow in their footsteps. When children do not do so, when they turn their backs on their parents' ideals and values, then the Divine Presence has indeed deserted the parents.

"I give the land you sojourn in to you and your offspring to come. . . . I will be your God. . . . As for you, you shall keep My covenant."

83

Rabbi Judah gave various interpretations of this. Among them: 1. If your children accept My Godhood, I will be their God and Patron. 2. If your children enter the Land, they accept my Godhood; if they do not enter, they do not accept. 3. If they accept circumcision they will enter the Land. Otherwise, they will not enter the land. Thus Joshua circumcised the Children of Israel when they entered the Land of Israel (Joshua 5:4) saying to them, "Do you think that you can enter the Land uncircumcised? Did not God say to Abraham, '*I give the land you sojourn in to you and your offspring to come*' on the condition that '*you shall keep My covenant* (of circumcision)'?" (Genesis Rabbah).

1) God may have chosen the Jewish people but the Jewish people must willingly choose God as well. The Lord will be our God only so long as we accept Him as God.

2) The love of the Jewish People for the Land of Israel is an integral part of the Religion of Israel. Those who sought to eliminate Eretz Yisroel from their thoughts and their prayers were not merely rejecting the Land but also a major part of their religion. Those who tried to establish a Judaism without Jewish Nationalism were falsifying the meaning of Judaism. Jewish Religion and Jewish Nationalism are one and inseparable.

3) What enabled the Jew to maintain his distinctive identity so that he was able "to enter the Land" after 2,000 years of homelessness? It was, in large measure, the ceremony of circumcision which maintained the distinctive identity of the Jew and thus made it possible for Jews to eventually reclaim their ancient homeland. While other aspects of the Jewish tradition may be ignored or discarded yet one remains a Jew, the ritual of circumcision is the *sine qua non* of identification as a member of the Jewish people.

From the words, "*As for you, you shall keep My covenant*" it can be deduced that circumcision performed by a non-Jew is not valid (Avodah Zarah 27a).

"As for you" means one like you. Hence it follows that only one who is himself circumcised may perform circumcision (Genesis Rabbah).

Many Jewish parents allow a doctor at the hospital to perform the circumcision and think they have thereby fulfilled the Jewish requirement. Circumcision, however, is not just an operation. It is a religious ritual that must be performed in a prescribed manner, to initiate a boy into the covenant of Abraham. In fact, the Hebrew word for circumcision is *Bris* which means covenant. Thus, if the circumcision is performed by a non-Jew it has no ritual significance and is not religiously valid.

"Such shall be the covenant, which you shall keep, between Me and you and your offspring to follow: every male among you shall be circumcised."

> Great is circumcision for it is one of the three covenants that God made between Himself and His creatures; the other two being the rainbow (Gen. 9:16) and the Sabbath (Exodus 31:17) — (Midrash HaGadol).

Each of these three covenants illustrates another aspect of God's concern for man. The rainbow symbolizes the importance of human life. Never again will God bring a Flood upon the world to destroy mankind. Man, on his part, must take every precaution to see that he does not unleash forces, atomic or otherwise, that will destroy the world.

The Sabbath symbolizes the importance of human dignity. Every man, no matter how humble, is entitled to a day of rest and relaxation. The Day of Rest on the seventh day emphasizes the fact that man, created on the sixth day, was created in the image of God and that his dignity as a human being created in God's image must be safeguarded.

Circumcision symbolizes God's special concern for the descendants of Abraham. The other two covenants apply to all men and indeed almost all faiths have adopted the concept of a Day of Rest but the covenant of circumcision applies only to Israel. It emphasizes the special relationship

85

that exists between God and Israel in addition to the relationship of God with all His creatures.

Where the father does not have his son circumcised the Jewish court is to have it done, for it is written, *"Every male among you shall be circumcised"* (Kiddushin 29a).

The Jewish community has an obligation to provide for the religious well-being of a Jewish child even if the parents refuse or neglect to do so. There are congregations that claim the right to deny a Jewish education or other religious benefits to a child whose parents refuse to meet their financial obligations to the synagogue. Actually, however, the Jewish community has a responsibility to the child and to Judaism regardless of the negative attitude displayed by the parents.

"You shall circumcise the flesh of your foreskin."

If his father or the Jewish court have not had him circumcised, it is his duty to have himself circumcised (Kiddushin 29a).

An individual does not have the right to cite the failure of his parents or of the Jewish community to provide adequately for his Jewish upbringing as justification for continuing to ignore his Jewish heritage as he matures. It is never too late to learn on one's own. Despite the lack of proper training in his youth, a Jew has a responsibility to learn about his heritage and to live a Jewish life.

"That shall be the sign of the covenant between Me and you. At the age of eight days every male among you throughout the generations shall be circumcised."

From the fact that the term *sign of the covenant* as well as the term *throughout the generations* are also used in regard to the Sabbath (Exodus 31:16), we can learn the law that circumcision takes precedence even over the Sabbath.

Here we are told, *at the age of eight days* and again in Leviticus we are told, *on the eighth day* (Lev.

12:3). Why the need for two verses telling us the same thing? One is needed to tell us that circumcision may not take place before the eighth day, the other to tell us that it should not be delayed beyond the eighth day (Shabbat 132b).

Many parents think that as long as the child is circumcised it makes no difference on what day the circumcision is performed. Therefore, they do not see anything wrong in having the circumcision performed on the third or fourth day at the hospital before the child is brought home, or in delaying the circumcision beyond the eighth day for the convenience of family or friends. In reality, however, it is so important that circumcision take place on the eighth day that even the Sabbath is suspended, and not only the Sabbath but even Yom Kippur. There is absolutely no valid reason for performing a circumcision *before* the eighth day, and the only valid reason for postponing it beyond the eighth day is the health of the child.

Sarah to Bear a Son

17:15-22

And God said to Abraham, "As for your wife Sarai, you shall not call her Sarai, but her name shall be Sarah.

The name Sarai or Sarah connotes a princess but Sarai is more limiting, meaning *"my* princess," only. Formerly she was a princess to her own people only. Now she is a princess to all mankind (Genesis Rabbah).

It was the mission of Abraham and Sarah to be a source of blessing not only to their own immediate family but to the entire world. The values and ideals they taught have enriched mankind spiritually. Their descendants, as well, have fulfilled that mission and have made great contributions to the welfare and advancement of all civilization.

Today, if only given an opportunity to live in peace and to develop their capacities to the fullest in their own land, they will prove to be an even greater source of blessing "to all mankind."

Upon being informed by God that Sarah would bear him a son, Abraham said to himself, *"Can a child be born to a man a hundred years old or can Sarah bear a child at ninety?"*

>When is a woman to be considered old? When she is called "Mother So and So" and does not mind (Genesis Rabbah).

Age is a subjective matter. A person is old when he or she feels old. One can be advanced in years and yet feel young and act young.

And Abraham said to God, "Oh that Ishmael might live by Your favor!"

>The skin of many a foal is stretched upon the back of the mother (Midrash HaChafetz).

Many a child has died while his parents yet live. Abraham prayed for the life of Ishmael because, unfortunately, it sometimes does happen that a child dies during the lifetime of the parent. The proverb is meant to connote that one cannot take anything for granted and that it cannot be assumed that a child will outlive the parent. We must be grateful for the blessings that we have. Abraham prayed for the welfare of Ishmael, being grateful to God that at least he had this one child. Often in our yearning for that which is not yet ours, we overlook the blessings that we do have and take them for granted.

>When Abraham exclaimed, *"Oh that Ishmael might live by Your favor"* what he hoped for was that Ishmael might repent so that he might attain life in the Future World (Midrash Hagadol).

Abraham was concerned not so much about the physical survival of his son, Ishmael, but about his spiritual survival. He was worried lest Ishmael go astray and die spiritually. Parents would be well advised to show more concern for the spiritual well-being of their children. Concern for their physical well-being is not enough.

God said, "Nevertheless, Sarah your wife shall bear you a son and you shall name him Isaac."

Of the three Patriarchs, only Isaac's name was never changed. Why? Because Abraham and Jacob received their names from their parents, while Isaac received his name from God Himself (Yerushalmi, Berachot 1).

The name "Isaac" comes from the root "to laugh." God said to Abraham and Sarah, "Because you made it something to laugh about, he shall be as his name implies" (Midrash HaGadol).

Laughter is a very healthy thing. Despite all the suffering he underwent, the Jew never lost the ability to laugh. This ability to laugh even in the midst of tears is indeed a God-given gift that has helped to sustain us throughout centuries of persecution.

"You shall name him Isaac because everybody will be rendered happy through him" (Midrash Aggadah).

The descendants of Isaac have been a source of happiness and blessing to mankind although unfortunately the peoples of the world have invariably been reluctant to acknowledge their indebtedness.

"As for Ishmael . . . he shall be the father of twelve chieftains."

Wherein lies the superiority of Sarah? She was the ancestress of twelve tribes but did not Ishmael also produce twelve chieftains? The truth is that these were chieftains (*Ne'si'im*) only in the sense in which the word is used in Proverbs 25:14, "As vapours (Ne'si'im) and wind without rain" (Genesis Rabbah).

89

In other words, the glory of the Ishmaelite chieftains would be transient and soon pass away while the glory of Israel would endure. In its long history, Israel has witnessed many nations more numerous and more powerful. They, however, have been *as vapours and wind*, soon passing off the stage of history while Israel continues to live and to flourish.

"I hereby bless him . . . but My covenant I will maintain with Isaac."

> God blessed Ishmael with the good things of this world: children, wealth, royalty, but the good things of the World to Come He has reserved for Isaac and his descendants (Midrash HaGadol).

Other nations may be more greatly blessed in a material sense but no nation has received the spiritual blessings that have been conferred upon the descendants of Isaac.

> When Isaac was born all were happy; the heavens and the earth, the sun and the moon, the stars and the planets. Why were they happy? Because had Isaac not been born, the world could not have endured (Tanchuma, Toledot 2).

The world endures through the merit of righteous men and women. Were there not Isaacs in the world, the world would be doomed to self-destruction.

And when He was done speaking with him, God was gone from Abraham.

> He who departs from his neighbor, whether he is greater or smaller, must ask his permission. We can learn this from Abraham. Abraham was talking to God when the ministering angels came to speak to him (18:2). Said he to them, "Let me take take leave first of the Divine Presence which is greater than you and then I will speak with you." When he had spoken with God all that was necessary, Abraham said to Him, "Master of the Universe, I

must speak to the angels." Said God to him, "Take leave in peace" as it is written, *God was gone from Abraham* (i.e. God took leave of Abraham with the latter's permission) (Genesis Rabbah).

From this incident we can learn a lesson in good manners. There is no excuse for impoliteness. No matter with whom one is speaking and what else one must do, one must be careful not to offend the feelings of others. It is a simple matter to observe the amenities of etiquette but it is not a light matter to refrain from doing so.

Abraham and Ishmael Circumcised

17:23-27

Then Abraham took his son Ishmael and all his homeborn slaves and all those he had bought, every male among Abraham's retainers, and he circumcised the flesh of their foreskins on that very day as God had spoken to him.

When God commanded Abraham about circumcision in his old age, Abraham did not hesitate nor did he pause to think about either the reward or the pain involved. Instead, he performed the *mitzvah* at once and for its own sake. The verse in Psalms, "that greatly delighteth in His commandments" (112:1) thus applies to Abraham who ran to perform God's commandments with joy and a willing spirit, not in order to receive a reward and not in order to avoid having misfortune come upon him, but out of love (Midrash HaGadol, Vayera).

Judaism commands us to observe God's commands not out of fear of punishment or expectation of reward but out of pure, disinterested love. "You must love the Lord your God with all your heart, and with all your soul, and with all your might," says the Torah (Deut. 6:5). Pirkei Avot admonishes us, "Do not be like servants who serve the master out of expectation of receiving a reward but be like servants who serve the master without any expectation of reward" (1:3). Pagans, also, sought to fulfill the wishes of their gods but they did so out of fear. Judaism was the first to introduce the concept of serving God out of love and not out of fear.

Thus Abraham and his son Ishmael were circumcised on that very day.

> He felt the pain and suffered in order that God might double his reward (Genesis Rabbah).

Only that which is attained through pain and suffering is truly appreciated and held dear. Jews throughout history have suffered pain and agony for the sake of their religion and this undoubtedly has made it more precious to them and contributed to their determination to cling to it at all costs.

CHAPTER 8

God Appears to Abraham

18:1

After Abraham's circumcision, *the Lord appeared to him by the terebinths of Mamre.*

He did so in order to perform the *mitzvah* of *Bikur Cholim* (visiting the sick) and thus set an example for all men to seek to emulate (Sotah 14a).

Visiting the sick is regarded by Judaism as one of the most important religious obligations. The Talmud declares that the reward for the fulfillment of this *mitzvah* is to be found both in this world and in the World to Come. Accordingly, we should never pass up an opportunity to bring cheer and comfort by paying a visit to one who is sick.

Why did God choose to appear to Abraham by the terebinths of Mamre? When God told Abraham to circumcise himself, he consulted his three friends, Aner, Eshkol and Mamre. Aner and Eshkol advised him against submitting to circumcision. Only Mamre rebuked him for hesitating even an instant to fulfill God's command. God, therefore, appeared to Abraham on the property of Mamre as a reward to Mamre for the good advice he had given to Abraham (Aggadot Breishit).

God does not ignore any meritorious act. In some way He demonstrates His appreciation and approval. God thus sets an example for us to emulate in our relationships with those who have been good to us.

But why did God choose to appear to Abraham by a terebinth? It was because Israel can be compared to a terebinth. Just as a terebinth, though it has dried up and its leaves have fallen, revives the moment it comes into contact with water, and produces buds and fruit, so it is with Israel. Though they may have descended to the lowest depths, when they will repent and the time of redemption will come, they will bloom and become radiant once again (Midrash HaGadol).

Jewish history has proven again and again that the Jewish people can revive and flourish when their fortunes seem at their very lowest ebb. Many a time, friend and foe alike have proclaimed the imminent demise of the Jewish people, only to be proven wrong again. The establishment of the State of Israel immediately after the slaughter of six million Jews during the Nazi Holocaust is but the most recent manifestation of the amazing resiliency of the Jew.

Abraham was sitting at the entrance of the tent as the day grew hot.

He was sitting there in order to see if there were any wayfarers passing by, so that he might invite them into his tent and extend to them his hospitality. He was particularly anxious because, due to his circumcision, two days had already passed without any wayfarers availing themselves of his hospitality. Abraham was afraid that travellers were avoiding his tent because they felt they would be imposing upon him (Midrash HaGadol).

Hachnasat Orchim, hospitality, is a most important *mitzvah.* From Father Abraham until our day Jews have gone to great lengths to fulfill this religious obligation. *Pirkei Avot* admonishes us, "Let your house be wide open, and treat the poor as members of your own family" (1:5). Like visiting the sick, hospitality to wayfarers is considered one of the commandments "whose fruit a man enjoys in this life while the principal remains for him to all eternity."

Abraham could have easily considered himself exempt from fulfilling the *mitzvah* of hospitality to strangers because he was engaged in fulfilling another very important *mitzvah*, that of circumcision; and the law is that "he who is engaged in the performance of a *mitzvah* is exempt from another." But Abraham was not looking for an excuse, or an easy way out. On the contrary, he eagerly sought out every opportunity to perform a good deed. Excuses are always at hand and come readily to mind for the one who seeks them, but the true disciple of Abraham does not look for excuses; rather he welcomes every opportunity to perform a *mitzvah*.

Job, who was also a most hospitable individual, prided himself on being the equal of Abraham in this regard. Said God to him, "Job, your hospitality cannot compare to Abraham's. You limited your hospitality to those who came to your door while Abraham on the third day after his circumcision was already sitting at the entrance to his tent looking for those who might be in need of hospitality (Avot d'Rabbi Nathan B, 14).

It is not enough to wait for those in need to come to us seeking our help. We must go forth and actively seek out those who are in need and are either too embarrassed to seek help or are unaware that help is available.

The Three Angels

18:2-8

Looking up, he saw three men standing near him. As soon as he saw them, he ran from the entrance of the tent to greet them.

In the text the word *Va'yar*, "and he saw," is repeated. The first time it is to be understood literally but the second time it indicates understanding. He understood that they were standing in one place and not approaching him because they did not want to trouble him. Therefore he ran to meet them (Rashi).

There are those who see but do not understand. They see the poverty and misery of the poor and underprivileged but they have no understanding of the feelings and sensitivities of these unfortunate people. Abraham understood the emotional needs of such individuals. He understood that a sensitive person finds it very painful to be the recipient of charity and that, therefore, the dispensing of help must be done in a tasteful, considerate manner that will not degrade or humiliate the recipient.

> Who were these three individuals? Michael, Gabriel and Raphael. Michael came to inform Sarah of the fact that she would bear a child; Raphael came to heal Abraham; Gabriel came to destroy the wicked city of Sodom (Baba Metzia 86a).
>
> It was necessary to send three angels because one angel is never permitted to perform more than one mission (Rashi).

Each person has his own specific contribution to make towards creating a better world. One need not feel called upon to solve single-handedly all the problems that beset mankind, for then he will fail miserably in all. Not even an angel could be successful trying to accomplish everything at once. A person seeking to be an angel of mercy can be far more effective by concentrating his efforts on one problem and doing all he can to achieve a solution to that problem.

> Abraham tended the needs of the three strangers though he thought them to be pagan Arabs (Kiddushin 32b).

The love and compassion of the Jew extends to non-Jews and even to those whose values and beliefs are diametrically opposed to his own. Witness the willingness of the Israelis after the Six Day War to throw open the medical facilities of the Hadassah hospital to Arabs who just a few days before were sworn to the annihilation of the Jewish state. If only Arab leaders would permit, Israel would eagerly prove once again the truth of the Talmudic statement that "he who has compassion upon his fellowman is of the descendants of Abraham our father, while he who does not have compassion upon his fellowman is not of the descendants of Abraham our father" (Be'zah 32b).

Bowing to the ground, he said, "My Lords (Adonai), if it please you, do not go on past your servant."

Abraham here uses the word *Adonai*, which is, of course, also the name of God. Therefore, there are those who maintain that Abraham was here in reality addressing God and not the strangers. He was asking God to excuse him so that he might tend to the needs of the wayfarers. From Abraham's action and God's acquiescence in it, we can learn that hospitality to wayfarers is even more important than receiving the *Shechinah*, the Divine Presence (Shevuot 35b).

See how different the nature of God is from the nature of man. It is the nature of man that an important personage would not tolerate an inferior saying to him, "Wait for me until I come to you." God, however, did not mind waiting for Abraham while the latter tended to the needs of the tired wayfarers (Shabbat 127a).

Whether a person really loves God or not can be ascertained from the way he treats his fellowman. Not only does God not require us to choose between our obligations to Him and our obligations to mankind; He insists that it is only by caring for the needs of humanity that we can truly honor Him.

"Let a little water be brought; bathe your feet and recline under the tree."

He bade them wash their feet because he suspected them of being Arabs who worship the dust of their feet (Baba Metzia 86b).

The fact that he suspected his guests of being pagans did not deter Abraham from extending his hospitality to them but it did cause him to take every precaution so that his home and family not be contaminated by pagan influences. As Jews we should by all means show friendship and hospitality to non-Jews but we have every right and duty to make certain that in extending such hospitality we do not affect adversely the religious practices and values of our own homes and families.

"And let me fetch a morsel of bread that you may refresh yourselves."

> Abraham only promised them *a morsel of bread* but he prepared a banquet for them. From this we learn that it is the nature of the righteous to promise little and do much in contrast to the wicked who promise much and do nothing at all (Baba Metzia 87a).

"Actions speak louder than words." One who performs does not need to promise. His actions will speak for him far more eloquently. Only the one who intends to do little or nothing has reason to loudly proclaim what he is going to accomplish.

> God repays man in accordance with his actions. Abraham offered bread to the strangers and in return God provided manna in the wilderness to his descendants for forty years (Mechilta, B'shallach, I).
>
> Abraham fetched water for his guests and God provided a bountiful well of water for his descendants in the wilderness (Tosefta, Sotah 4).

We never know when a good deed we have performed may become an unexpected source of blessing to ourselves or our children. Conversely, a thoughtless act or evil deed may come back to haunt us in a most unexpected manner. A long time ago the wise Kohelet observed, "Cast thy bread upon the waters, for thou shalt find it after many days" (Ecc. 11:1).

The angels replied, "Do as you have said."

> Of course, angels neither eat nor drink. Why then did they accept Abraham's hospitality? They did

so in order to teach us that a guest should not refuse his host's hospitality and that one shows respect to a person by accepting (Midrash Habiur).

Just as it is incumbent upon a person to offer hospitality, so it is incumbent upon one to accept the offer graciously. It is just as important to be a gracious guest as it is to be a gracious host.

Abraham hastened into the tent to Sarah, and said, "Quick, three measures of choice flour! Knead and make cakes!" Then Abraham ran to the herd.

See how eager Abraham was to perform a mitzvah (Midrash Ha'chefetz). The righteous act with speed (Midrash Aggadah).

Well could we learn from Abraham. Generally, when it comes to the performance of a *mitzvah,* we feel no sense of urgency. We feel we can do it when we get around to it. Our Sages, however, tell us, "When an opportunity to perform a *mitzvah* presents itself, do it at once." The adage of the great Hillel "If not now, when" (Avot 1:14) applies to the performance of any good deed. Procrastination is the deadly enemy of good intentions. Perhaps this is the reason why, although ordinarily a blessing is recited before the performance of a *mitzvah,* we do not recite a blessing before giving charity or helping another human being; to indicate that nothing should be permitted to intervene between the need to be of assistance and the fulfillment of the responsibility.

Sarah was to be found in her tent. The verse in Psalms, "All glorious is the king's daughter within the palace" (45:14) means that it is the glory of a woman to be within her own home, as is exemplified by Sarah who was to be found in her tent (Pesikta Zutrati).

Mother Sarah is held up as an example to be emulated by all Jewish women. In our modern age, women have been emancipated and are able to have careers and to participate in all spheres of community endeavor. Insofar as Women's

Lib has encouraged women to fully realize all their potentialities it has performed a service but unfortunately it has also led some women to disparage the still indispensable role they should play in the home. Being a housewife should not be something to be ashamed of, as is the case with so many modern women. The role of the woman within "her own tent" is still the most important and worthwhile role that she can possibly play and should never be disparaged or downgraded.

> Abraham had many servants but he himself *ran to the herd* to fetch the calf. Whatever Abraham personally did for the angels, God Himself did for Abraham's children. Abraham personally *ran to the herd* and so God personally provided quails for his descendants in the wilderness (Numbers 11:31), so that they might have meat to eat (Baba Metzia 86b).

We tend to rely too much on servants and subordinates to perform our good deeds for us. It is always easier to write a check than it is to give of oneself. But from Abraham we should learn the necessity for personal involvement. Whatever we do personally is of far greater significance than that which we do by proxy.

Abraham *took a calf tender and choice and gave it to a servant-boy who hastened to prepare it.*

> The calf that Abraham selected was both *tender and choice* because whatever he did, he did in a magnanimous fashion. Whoever does things in a magnanimous manner is a true disciple of Abraham (Avot d'Rabbi Natan 13).

There are those who give charity or provide hospitality but do it grudgingly and as cheaply as they possibly can get away with. From Abraham, however, we should learn to give of the best that is ours and to do it with a full heart.

> Who was that servant-boy? His own son Ishmael whom he wanted to train in the performance of good deeds (Genesis Rabbah).

There can be no substitute for actual experience in performing good deeds. Unfortunately, modern parents have a tendency to try to spare their children any unnecessary effort with the result that the children have little or no opportunity to gain experience in the performance of good deeds. We should realize that the effort we spare them may well be at the expense of their character. Instead of merely preaching to our children the virtues of charity and kindness, it would be far better if we enabled them to have actual experience by giving charity from their own allowance, and by requiring them to exert themselves in the performance of deeds of loving-kindness.

He took curds and milk and the calf that had been prepared and set these before them; and he waited on them under the tree as they ate.

> We are told that the angels ate but of course we know that angels do not eat. What is meant, therefore, is that they appeared to be eating and drinking. The angels when on earth pretended to eat; Moses, while on High to receive the Torah, refrained from eating. From this we learn that a person should not deviate from the custom of the locality (Baba Metzia 86b).

Where matters of principle are involved one should not hesitate to be a non-conformist and to stand alone if necessary. But where no principle is involved, non-conformity just for the sake of being different is not only no virtue but a defect. The adage "When in Rome do as the Romans" has validity because one should not violate the feelings of people for no reason. Wisely does the Midrash state, "When you come into a city, guide yourself according to its customs" (Genesis Rabbah 48).

> From the fact that Abraham personally served three strangers whom he believed to be pagan Arabs we can learn that even the great should not be ashamed to personally serve the lowly. When the President of the Sanhedrin, Rabban Gamliel, invited

his colleagues to a party celebrating the circumcision of his son, he sought to personally pour wine for them. Rabbi Elazar did not want to permit him to do so, feeling that it was beneath the dignity of a great Prince of Israel such as Rabban Gamliel. Rabbi Joshua, however, permitted the host to pour for him. Rabbi Elazar rebuked him, "Joshua, how can we permit ourselves to be seated while Rabban Gamliel stands over us and serves us?" Rabbi Joshua, however, replied that it was perfectly proper. "Did not Abraham, who was one of the great men of the world, personally minister to the angels even though he thought them to be pagan Arabs? If Abraham could serve those he believed to be pagan Arabs, certainly Rabban Gamliel can serve us" (Kiddushin 32b).

Abraham's humility and eagerness to serve personally even those of low station in life, set an example for his descendants to follow. We should never feel that it is beneath our dignity to be gracious to, or to personally assist, any human being.

Ultimately, Abraham came to realize that his visitors were angels and he prolonged his meal with them in order that he might be able to benefit fully from the opportunity of dining with great men. From Abraham's behaviour we can learn that a person should always seek to spend his time at the table with scholars so that he might learn from them words of Torah, but should seek to avoid dining with ignoramuses, for before long they will be gossiping about him (Yalkut Shimoni).

The company we keep at the dinner table is indeed important. Even when dining with our own family we should seek to keep the conversation on a high intellectual and moral plane, instead of indulging in petty gossip and small talk. Too often, we overlook the importance of the dinner table as an educational and inspirational instrument.

Sarah Learns She Will Give Birth

18:9-16

They said to him (Aylav), "Where is your wife Sarah?"
And he replied, "There, in the tent."

Why did they have to ask? Being angels did they not know that she was in the tent? Of course they knew, but they asked the question nevertheless in order to endear her to her husband (Baba Metzia 87a).

The purpose of the question was simply to enable Abraham to take pride in the modesty of his wife who was tending her womanly chores in the tent. A considerate person will frequently ask a question not so much to elicit information but to give the one asked an opportunity to discuss his family, his accomplishments, his ambitions in life.

In the Hebrew text there are dots over three of the four letters in the Hebrew word *Aylav*. Why? The Torah here gives us a lesson in manners, teaching us that correct behaviour calls for a man to always inquire of his host concerning the well-being of the members of his family (Baba Metzia 87a).

There are people who neglect the amenities and are disdainful of politeness and good manners, considering them to be superfluous at best and hypocritical at worst. They are wrong, however. Civility and simple good manners are important and should not be disregarded.

When Sarah, who was listening at the tent door, heard the angel tell Abraham that she would have a son, she *laughed to herself, saying, "Now that I am withered, am I to have enjoyment—with my husband so old?" Then the Lord said to Abraham, "Why did Sarah laugh, saying, 'Shall I in truth bear a child, old as I am?' "*

Sarah had referred to her husband's old age not just to her own. Why then should Scripture here

103

deviate from the truth and omit reference to Sarah's remark that her husband was too old to father a child? God did not hesitate to omit part of the truth in order to preserve marital harmony between Abraham and his wife, for had Abraham been told that Sarah considered him too old to father a child, he would have been offended (Baba Metzia 87a).

Truth is of course a great virtue. In fact, our Sages tell us that "the seal of the Almighty is truth" (Shabbat 55a). Nevertheless, the demand for truthfulness should never be used as an excuse for brutal frankness that wounds and offends. It is permissible to withhold some information or even to tell a white lie if by so doing we can spare a person's feelings and especially if we can thereby prevent marital discord. Exclaiming to a friend, "Do you know what so and so said about you?" can never be justified on the grounds that "I must tell the truth no matter whom it hurts."

The men set out from there and looked down toward Sodom, Abraham walking with them to see them off.

When the angels departed, Abraham accompanied them on their way. As the proverb has it, "When you have given your guest food and drink, escort him also" (Genesis Rabbah).

When one does a good deed he should see it through to its completion and not leave it even partially undone. A person can undo much of the good he has already accomplished by failing to put the finishing touches on his good deed.

A man is repaid in accordance with his own actions. Abraham accompanied the angels on their way and as a reward God accompanied his children in the wilderness for forty years (Mechilta, B'shallach 1).

Invariably, kindless is repaid by kindness just as cruelty is repaid with cruelty. The way we act towards others generally determines the way others act towards us.

104

God Informs Abraham of His Intentions

18:17-18

Having decided to destroy the wicked city of Sodom, God said, *"Shall I hide from Abraham what I am about to do?"*

Why does God feel it necessary to inform Abraham of His intentions? Because having already promised Abraham, *"I give all the land that you see to you and your offspring"* (13:15), God feels that it would be wrong to destroy cities that have been promised to Abraham, without his knowledge (Tanchuma).

God does not use His omnipotence to run roughshod over the rights, however tenuous, of any human being. Certainly, then, we must scrupulously take into consideration the rights and feelings of others before utilizing whatever power we may possess. We must never conduct ourselves as if we accept the pernicious doctrine of "Might makes Right."

Another reason God informed Abraham of His intentions was because He wanted Abraham to plead on behalf of the wicked inhabitants of Sodom (Tanchuma).

Every accused is entitled to a defense attorney who will defend him to the utmost of his ability. Only thus can the cause of justice be served. In fact, the Talmud tells us that a person accused of a capital offense cannot be convicted unless there is at least one member of the Sanhedrin who is ready to plead his cause. No matter how depraved the crime or how unsavory the criminal, there should be someone to plead for him. Certainly, the lawyer who agrees to defend an unpopular client should not be hounded for it; rather should he be applauded for serving the purposes of justice.

For I Have Singled Him Out

18:19

Speaking of Abraham, God declares, *"For I have singled him out that he may instruct his children and his posterity to keep the way of the Lord, to do righteousness (Zedakah) and justice (Mishpat) in order that the Lord may bring about for Abraham what He has promised him."*

The righteous not only do what is right but they also instruct others to do that which is right, in contrast to the wicked who not only sin themselves but also cause others to stumble (Midrash HaGadol).

The way we live is bound to have an impact upon others. A righteous person by his life and his teachings can be a profound influence for good upon all those with whom he comes in contact.

Abraham left instructions to *his children and his posterity.* Happy are the righteous in that before they depart this world they instruct their children concerning the Torah, as did Abraham (Midrash Tannaim, Devarim).

In fulfillment of this injunction to instruct one's posterity, there has grown up a whole literature of Ethical Wills. Long before their deaths, pious Jews would prepare instructions for their descendants. Having very little to bequeath to their children in the way of material things, Jews took great pains to convey ethical and moral values in their last wills and testaments.

What is considered *the way of the Lord?* To do righteousness and justice (Tanchuma, Shoftim).

From the very beginning, Judaism insisted that *the way of the Lord* was not merely worship of God or the observance of ritual but *to do righteousness and justice.* That Abraham was the first to give to the world the idea of Monotheism is not quite as important as the fact that he originated the idea of Ethical Monotheism, of a God who demanded of His followers righteousness and justice in all their acts and deeds.

Three characteristics distinguish the descendants of Abraham. They are compassionate, modest and performers of deeds of loving-kindness. Anyone possessing these three characteristics is worthy of attaching himself to the Jewish people. Performing deeds of loving-kindness is a distinguishing characteristic of the descendants of Abraham, for it is written *that he may instruct his children and his posterity to keep the way of the Lord, to do righteousness and justice* (Yevamot 79a).

The uniqueness of the Jewish people lies not in any racial characteristic, but in the moral superiority that has always characterized the Jew. Any human being who possesses these moral characteristics is considered worthy of becoming a Jew. However, a righteous individual need not convert to Judaism to achieve a place in the World to Come, for "the righteous of all nations have a share in the World to Come."

What does *to do righteousness and justice* refer to? One Sage refers it to consoling the bereaved; another to visiting the sick (Genesis Rabbah).

Being righteous and just connotes more than merely refraining from harming others, more even than helping in a physical or material sense. It also entails being kind and sympathetic in time of sickness or sorrow. Consoling the bereaved and visiting the sick may not ordinarily entail financial sacrifice but they are *mitzvot* of supreme importance, nevertheless. Psychological and spiritual uplift in time of need can be even more crucial to a person's well-being than material sustenance.

The word *Zedakah* "righteousness" is also the Hebrew word for "charity". Great is charity, for throughout history whoever has given it has been praised by God for it. Our early ancestors merited

107

both this world and the World to Come only because they accustomed themselves to give charity. Abraham, Isaac and Jacob, Moses, Aaron, David and Solomon were all praised because of *Zedakah*. Of Abraham it says, *"For I have singled him out . . . to do Zedakah"* (Seder Eliyahu Zuta).

It is significant that in Hebrew the word for charity is the same as the word for righteousness. It indicates that what is ordinarily referred to as charity is equated by Judaism with doing that which is right and just. The relief of poverty is an act of simple justice not of benevolence. The poor are entitled to food, clothing and shelter as of right and not as objects of philanthropy. Thus the Torah ordains that the gleanings of a field, the corners of a field, and that which is overlooked by the farmer in his field are all legally the property not of the owner of the field but of the poor.

> *Righteousness (charity) and justice.* What kind of justice includes charity? Compromise! Compromise is superior to unbending justice (Midrash HaGadol).

Our prime interest should be the establishment of peace and harmony between disputing parties. The demands of justice must always be tempered by the need to create the kind of harmony that will prevent the recurrence of constant squabbling and bickering. A compromise which is acceptable to both sides though not entirely satisfactory to either, is therefore preferable to a decision which leaves one side spoiling for revenge.

> Abraham instructed his children to keep the way of the Lord *in order that the Lord may bring about for Abraham what He has promised him*. Notice that the text does not say *that the Lord may bring about* for Abraham's family, but for Abraham himself. From this we can see that whoever is able to raise up a righteous son is considered as if he has not died (Genesis Rabbah; cf Rashi).

We live on in our children. If we are able to raise up righteous children, who will carry on our ideals and values, then it can be truly said after we are gone that we have not died. When we remember our parents at *Yizkor* time we would do well to remember also that only by carrying on the ideals and values of our parents do we give them life.

The Sins of Sodom

18:20-21

Then the Lord said, "The outrage of Sodom and Gomorah is so great, and their sin so grave! I will go down to see whether they have acted altogether according to the out-cry that has come to me."

What cry did God hear? It was the cry of a young girl. She had taken pity on a poor stranger who was dying of hunger and supplied him with food. When her "crime" was discovered, for to the Sodomites it was indeed a crime to offer any assistance to a stranger, she was put to a most cruel death. It was the cry of this unfortunate girl that God could not ignore (Pirkei d'Rabbi Eliezer 25).

God can overlook many failings and shortcomings of man but He cannot overlook and ignore oppression of the poor, the weak and the defenseless. Any society, therefore, that oppresses the weak, or that passively permits such oppression, is courting inevitable destruction.

Perversion of justice by those who should have been its guardians characterized Sodom. There were four judges in Sodom bearing such names as Liar, Awful Liar, Forger and Perverter of Justice. If a man assaulted his neighbor's wife and bruised her, these judges would say to the husband, "You must give her to him that she may become pregnant for you." If a man cut off the ear of his neighbor's ass, the judges would rule, "Give the ass to him until the ear grows back." If a man wounded his neighbor,

109

they would say to the victim, "Pay your assailant a fee for bleeding you" and so forth. This was the nature of justice in the courts of Sodom (Sanhedrin 109b).

There is hope for a society, no matter how much crime and lawlessness there may be, so long as the courts of law remain staunch defenders of justice. But when the courts are corrupt and there is no place one who has been wronged can go to seek a redress of grievances, then that society is doomed. In our country, the courts, and particularly the Supreme Court, have come under considerable criticism for insisting that all the safeguards of the law be scrupulously adhered to even if it means that the guilty may sometimes go free. It is our duty to support the courts in their insistence that the rights of all accused must be protected at all costs. Hysterics and vindictiveness must not replace law and reason in the courtroom. A strong, independent, incorruptible judiciary is the best safeguard against tyranny.

The Sodomites devised special devices to make it impossible for any stranger to dwell in their midst. For example, they had beds upon which travellers slept. If the guest was too long, they shortened him by cutting off his feet. If he was too short, they stretched him out (Sanhedrin 109b).

The Sodomites insisted upon strict conformity. They were suspicious of all strangers because they could not tolerate anybody who was different. In their society everybody was expected to look alike, dress alike, act alike and think alike. The pressures for conformity, of course, are present in every society, including our own. It takes a great deal of courage to be a non-conformist and to refuse to be confined to the measurements of "the bed of Sodom." If our society considers itself to be morally superior to Sodom, then we must be willing to tolerate and even welcome non-conformity and not seek to impose the same values and ideals upon everyone. It is easy enough to advocate freedom of speech and expression for those whose opinions are popular or with whom we personally agree. However, the real test of whether we believe in free speech or not is whether we are willing to fight for the right of the person with whom we disagree to speak his mind without fear of punishment or harassment.

The hatred and suspicion of strangers that characterized Sodom had its origin in the material blessings which God had lavished upon them. They said, "Since bread comes forth out of our earth, and our earth also produces gold-dust, why should we admit outsiders who come only to deplete our wealth. Let us do away with the practice of people coming into our land" (Sanhedrin 109b).

Is this not reminiscent of the attitude of so many Americans who seek to shut the gates of America in the face of would-be immigrants to this country? Is not the quota system of immigration, in some measure, a manifestation of this spirit of Sodom? There is a reluctance on the part of many who came to these shores in one era to share with those who seek to come in the next generation. In fact, the opposition to Foreign Aid for underdeveloped nations is also rooted in the spirit of Sodom, in the refusal to share the material blessings that God has lavished upon us with those who are less fortunate.

Why was it necessary for God *to go down to see* the wickedness for Himself? Did not God in His omniscience know for a certainty that the Sodomites were wicked? God, of course, did not need to *go down to see* but He did so as an example to judges that they not condemn an accused in a capital case unless there are eyewitnesses (Rashi).

God wanted to teach by example not only judges in a court of law but each and every one of us that we not accuse anyone of wrongdoing on the basis of hearsay. Before we accuse and condemn we must *go down to see* for ourselves whether the accusation is true or not. Too often, we are prone to believe any accusation that is hurled, rationalizing that "where there is smoke there must be fire." If only we would insist upon "seeing for ourselves" before believing and repeating vicious charges, many an innocent person would be spared untold suffering and anguish.

Another reason for God "going down to see" instead of immediately executing judgment upon Sodom was His desire to give them the opportunity to do *Teshuva* and repent (Genesis Rabbah).

Even the most wicked are given the opportunity to change their ways. Witness Jonah's mission to the wicked inhabitants of Ninevah who did indeed repent and were thus spared destruction. The power of Repentance is very great. Unfortunately, however, the ones in need of it most, utilize it least.

Actually, the real prosperity of Sodom lasted for only 52 years and for the last 25 of these God made the mountains to tremble and brought all kinds of terror upon them in order that they might reform, yet they did not (Genesis Rabbah).

Perhaps the social upheavals taking place in our own country; the riots, demonstrations, violence and crime, are God's way of warning us that we must reform our society if it is to survive. Yet we disregard the warnings and blithely assume that the prosperity our country enjoys is destined to continue forever despite the injustices we permit to exist. God grant that we awaken in time and thus avoid the fate of Sodom which perished because it refused to heed the all-too-apparent danger signals.

Abraham's Plea for Sodom

18:22-33

Upon hearing of God's intention to destroy Sodom, *Abraham came forward and said, "Will You indeed (Ha'af) sweep away the innocent along with the guilty?"*

"Coming forward" can mean for battle, for conciliation or for prayer. What Abraham said was, "I come, whether it be for battle, conciliation or prayer" (Genesis Rabbah).

Abraham was ready to use every weapon at his command to achieve his righteous purpose. If conciliation would suffice, that would be fine. Prayer would always be in order. But if justice could be secured in no other way, he was ready to do battle for what he believed. Jacob, also, confronted by the army of his brother Esau, relied first upon concilation and prayer but also prepared himself for battle if all else failed. We Jews believe in peace but we do not believe in pacifism at all costs. No effort should be spared in trying to achieve a righteous goal peacefully, but as a last resort sometimes it is necessary to go out and do battle for what one believes.

Abraham argued before God, *"Will you indeed (Ha'af) sweep away the innocent along with the guilty?"* The word *Af* also means anger. Abraham argued thusly, "You have mastery over Your anger; anger does not have mastery over You. Would You destroy in your anger the righteous and the wicked? Not only are You refusing to spare the guilty because of the innocent but You will also be destroying the innocent together with the guilty. A human being is ruled by his anger but the Almighty rules anger" (Genesis Rabbah).

There are times when anger and indignation are essential. The person who is never indignant about anything is a person who does not care about the social injustice and the suffering that abound in the world. But anger must not hold sway over us to the point where we are its slave and cannot control our wrath. We should, in imitation of God, seek to have mastery over our anger at all times. Even when it is righteous indignation we must know how to channel it into constructive purposes rather than simply striking out blindly and seeking to destroy all in our path.

"What if there should be fifty innocent within the city; will You then wipe out the place and not forgive it for the sake of the innocent fifty who are in it?"

113

Why did he begin with fifty? Because in all there were 5 cities involved. Abraham hoped that there would be 10 righteous individuals in each of the 5 cities for he knew that God does not ignore the prayer of a community (and ten constitute a *Minyan,* the minimum needed for communal prayer) (Midrash HaChafetz).

Individual prayer, praiseworthy as it is, is no substitute for *Tefillah B'tzibur,* communal prayer. When a Jew prays as part of the community in public worship he is helping to preserve the Jewish people and his prayer is far more efficacious than if he were to pray alone.

From Abraham's plea we can also learn that if there are 50 righteous men in the world, the world will endure through the merit of their righteousness (Pirkei d'Rabbi Eliezer).

A few truly righteous individuals have it in their power to preserve mankind. Jewish legend has developed the idea of the *Lamed Vav,* 36 righteous men upon whose goodness the continued existence of the world depends. These 36 individuals are extremely modest and their identity is unknown. They may live as ignorant, poverty-stricken people and they are scattered throughout the world but in time of trouble they succeed in averting the calamity that impends.

"Far be it from You to do such a thing, to bring death upon the innocent as well as the guilty, so that innocent and guilty fare alike."

Job said almost the identical thing, "It is all one; therefore, I say, He destroyeth the innocent and the wicked" (Job 9:22). Yet Abraham was rewarded for what he said and Job was punished. Why? The difference was in the way they said it. Abraham was saying, "Surely God would not do such an unjust thing." Job on the other hand was flatly denying God's justice (Genesis Rabbah).

Frequently, the true significance of our words is determined not by *what* we say but by the manner in which we

114

say it and the purpose we have in mind. Criticism, even of God and certainly of man, is permissible provided it is done to achieve a constructive purpose and out of love; but when it is purely destructive, with no purpose in mind except to condemn and to find fault, it is not permissible and must be avoided at all costs.

> Abraham pleaded with God, "You have promised never again to bring a Flood upon the world. Are You now seeking to evade Your promise? Are You saying that a deluge of water You will not bring but a deluge of fire You will bring? If so, You have really evaded Your promise" (Genesis Rabbah).

Technically, God would not be breaking His promise if He destroyed the world by fire, as His promise concerned only a deluge of water. But being technically honest, or technically within the law, while getting around the law through all sorts of technicalities, is most improper. We must seek to keep not only the letter of the law but its spirit as well and not evade the consequences of promises we have made by resorting to technicalities or semantics.

"Far be it from You! Shall not the Judge of all the earth deal justly?"

> Abraham argued with God, "If You want the world to exist, You cannot have strict justice. If You insist upon strict justice, the world cannot exist. You, however, want to hold the rope at both ends. You want the world to exist and at the same time You want strict justice. You must forego a little or else the world will be unable to exist" (Genesis Rabbah).

Standing upon principle is a wonderful thing but sometimes by refusing to bend even a little we lose everything. A willingness to compromise, to give in a little, is often essential if one is to achieve anything at all. Our Sages tell us that the Second Temple was destroyed because of one person's insistence that there be no compromise whatsoever; that every detail of the sacrificial law must be scrupu-

115

lously observed even if it meant arousing the ire of Rome and consequently the destruction of the Temple. Compromise is not identical with surrender. Would that the leaders of the world could learn this lesson before they destroy the world for the sake of what they maintain to be their principles. Also, how much happier each one of us would be if we took to heart this lesson in our relationships with family and friends.

> Said Abraham to the Almighty, "In the case of a human judge, an appeal can be made to a higher authority. Shall You, because no appeal can be made from Your judgment, not do justice? Because there is no one to veto You, shall You not act justly?" (Genesis Rabbah).

The more power a person has, the greater is his obligation to use it in a responsible fashion. Leaders of government and business, as well as parents and teachers who expect obedience from children and students, have an obligation to take to heart this admonition of Abraham and not use their authority lightly or arbitrarily.

And the Lord answered, "If I find within the city of Sodom fifty innocent ones I will forgive the whole place for their sake." Abraham spoke up saying, "Here I venture to speak to the Lord, I who am but dust and ashes."

> Said God to Israel, "I love you because even when I bestow greatness upon you, you humble yourselves before Me. I bestowed greatness on Abraham and he exclaimed, 'I am but dust and ashes.' And so it was with Moses and Aaron, with David and with others upon whom I bestowed greatness" (Chullin 89a).

By consulting with Abraham, God had bestowed greatness upon him, yet Abraham remained modest and humble. There are those who as soon as they achieve a position of prominence become swelled up with their own importance. "Conceit is God's gift to little men." The truly great man, like Abraham, remains modest and unassuming before God and before his fellow man. From Abraham's reaction, we learn how a Jew should react to fame or fortune. A humble spirit is one of the three distinguishing characteristics of a disciple of Abraham, our Father.

"What if the fifty innocent should lack five? Will You destroy the whole city for want of five?"

> Why did Abraham limit himself at first to asking about the lack of only five? The Torah here teaches us proper behaviour. When one comes to the king with a request, he should begin with something small. If he finds that the king is gracious to him and grants his request, then he can ask for what he really wants (Midrash HaChafetz).

When one is dependent upon the goodwill of others it is better not to make demands or requests that seem to be extravagant and therefore are likely to be rejected out of hand. It is often possible to achieve much more by limiting oneself at the outset to modest requests and establishing the kind of a relationship that will make possible the attaining of much more later on. Thus, moderate leaders of underprivileged groups are generally far more effective in bettering the lot of their people than are extremist leaders whose demands serve only to antagonize those who are in a position to help.

Abraham continues to bargain with God, finally asking, *"What if ten should be found there?" And He answered, "I will not destroy, for the sake of the ten."*

> Why did Abraham ultimately limit himself to asking about ten? It was because he thought that there were ten righteous individuals there; Lot and his wife, Lot's four daughters and four sons-in-law. Also, he did not ask God to spare the city for less, because he knew that in the Generation of the Flood there had been eight righteous individuals and yet they had not been able to save their generation (Genesis Rabbah).

> From the fact that God agreed that *"I will not*

destroy, for the sake of the ten" we learn that whenever there are ten righteous people in a place, the place will be spared for their sake (Pirkei d'Rabbi Eliezer 25).

A few righteous people can help to save an entire society. But in order to be really effective these righteous individuals must be able to band together in a fellowship of their own. Each one by himself can achieve little but working together as a group, signified by the number ten, they can achieve a great deal in redirecting the much larger community of which they are a part.

When the Lord had finished speaking to Abraham He departed; and Abraham returned to his place.

As long as the defense attorney is pleading the case of his client, the judge patiently waits. Only when the defense attorney falls silent is the judge free to go on his way (Genesis Rabbah).

God listened patiently and attentively as long as Abraham had anything to say on behalf of Sodom. The processes of justice often seem very long and drawn out. Nevertheless, as long as the defense has something to say, as long as there is another avenue of appeal still open, we should not seek in any way to hasten the judicial process by limiting the right of the defense to plead its case. There can be no shortcut to justice.

CHAPTER 9

Lot's Hospitality

19:1-3

The two angels arrived in Sodom in the evening as Lot was sitting in the gate of Sodom.

Three angels came to visit Abraham; now there are only two. God had sent three angels, each to perform a specific mission; one to inform Sarah she would give birth, one to save Lot and one to destroy Sodom. Just as one angel does not perform two missions, so two angels are not needed to perform one mission. Once the angel Michael had completed his mission of informing Sarah he departed, and the other two, Gabriel and Raphael, went on to perform *their* missions. That is why only two angels are now mentioned rather than three (Tanchuma, Buber).

When one has completed his task, it is better to remove oneself from the scene rather than to hang around aimlessly. Too often, people do not know how to make a graceful departure and move on to other things when the task they have undertaken is accomplished. Leaders in particular must be able to sense when the time has come for them to make way gracefully for new leadership with new ideas to meet new conditions.

Why are they here referred to as angels whereas when they first appeared to Abraham they had been called men (18:2)? Before they performed their mission they were called men; having performed their mission of informing Sarah they are now called angels (Genesis Rabbah).

It is only after one has accomplished something that he deserves any praise or accolades. Sometimes a person is hailed as a great "savior" before he has accomplished anything and turns out to be a terrible disappointment. It is only after a man has produced and can be judged on his achievements that he merits our acclaim.

The angels did not reach Sodom until evening even though they had departed from Abraham at noon. What took them so long? Being angels, and therefore able to travel with the speed of lightning, surely they could have reached Sodom much earlier, had they so desired. But the fact is that they were Angels of Mercy and, therefore, they purposely delayed, thinking that perhaps Abraham would be able to find some merit in the inhabitants of Sodom so that the city need not be destroyed. It was only after Abraham was unable to do so that *the two angels arrived in Sodom in the evening* (Genesis Rabbah).

Although it is improper to delay the performance of a *mitzvah* for even a moment, it is permissible and even desirable to delay punishment as long as possible in the hope that the individual may come to his senses or some merit may be found in him, and thus the need for punishment be obviated. Sometimes it may seem that we are too patient with law-breakers and violent demonstrators but it is better to be too patient than too impatient. Perhaps, given time and patience, the issue can be resolved without the use of force and the resulting bitterness and permanent alienation.

Why was Lot sitting in the gate at night? When Lot first came to Sodom he made it his business to be hospitable to strangers, as he had learned from his uncle, Abraham. However, the Sodomites announced that anyone caught providing as much as a slice of bread to a poor man would be burned to death for the crime. Therefore, being afraid to provide hospitality by day, Lot did so by night. That is why he was sitting in the gate of Sodom at nighttime (Pirkei d'Rabbi Eliezer 25).

Because Lot grew up in the home of Abraham, he learned to be like him. Thus, Solomon said, "Train up a child in the way he should go, and even when he is old, he will not depart from it" (Prov. 22:6) — (Tanchuma, Buber).

The habits, good or bad, that are ingrained when one is young are difficult to break. Lot was willing to risk his life to provide hospitality to strangers because this is what he had learned as a child growing up in the home of his uncle. It was unthinkable to him not to offer such hospitality even though he now lived in an environment which regarded such kindness as a criminal act. A person's character throughout life is profoundly affected by the examples set for him and the habits he acquires even in earliest childhood. Parents ignore this fact at the peril of their child's moral development.

Said Lot to them *"Please, my lords, turn aside to your servant's house to spend the night and bathe your feet."*

What did Lot mean by the phrase *"turn aside to your servant's house"?* What he meant was, "Come to me by a circuitous route, so that you not be seen coming to me" (Genesis Rabbah).

Lot had to perform the *mitzvah* in secret out of fear of the inhabitants of Sodom. What a tragic indictment of a society when a person must resort to subterfuge in order to fulfill the dictates of his conscience! This was the lot of the Marranos who had to observe their religion in secret ever fearful that the dreaded Inquisition might discover them in the act of committing the "crime" of remaining loyal to their heritage. Unfortunately, it remains the lot of many Jews and others to this day.

Abraham had asked them to wash first and then enjoy his hospitality (18:4). Lot, however, invited them to first *spend the night* and then *bathe your feet*. The reason for the difference is that Abraham was particular about the pollution of idolatry whereas Lot had no objection to it (Genesis Rabbah).

121

Lot had acquired some of Abraham's virtues such as extending hospitality to strangers but, unlike Abraham, he was not troubled by the evil of the society in which he lived. We who are the descendants of Abraham must never allow our consciences to be assuaged by certain good deeds we perform while remaining oblivious to, and unmoved by, the evils and injustices which pollute the society of which we are an integral part.

But they said, "No, we will spend the night in the square."

Why did they at first decline Lot's offer although they had not refused Abraham? From this one can learn that although you may refuse an ordinary person, you may not refuse a great person (Genesis Rabbah).

Respect for a man of learning, piety or distinction requires accepting even his offer of aid and assistance. To refuse a distinguished personage's offer of hospitality because of reluctance to inconvenience him reveals a mistaken sense of deference and respect.

Finally they accepted and Lot *prepared a feast for them and baked unleavened bread.*

In the case of Abraham's hospitality, it was his wife Sarah who baked cakes. Here it was Lot himself who *baked unleavened bread* for his guests. His wife refused to bring them even a little salt (Pesikta Zutrati).

Lot's wife was a true daughter of Sodom. She sought to deny hospitality to the strangers, begrudging them even a little salt. Happy is the man whose wife is a true "helpmate" to him, sharing his values and ideals. Unhappy is the man whose wife, like Lot's, does not share his values and refuses to cooperate in his efforts to benefit his fellowman.

The Anger of the Sodomites

19:4-11

They had not yet lain down, when the townspeople, the men of Sodom, young and old—all the people to the last man— surrounded the house.

> The purpose of the repetition here is to emphasize that not one of them objected (Genesis Rabbah).

All the inhabitants of the city, leadership and masses alike, were wicked and depraved. Aside from Lot, there were no decent people in the city and God was thus completely justified in rejecting Abraham's plea on its behalf. Even if there were citizens of Sodom who in their hearts did not completely approve of what was being done, they too were deserving of punishment because "they went along with the crowd" and not one of them objected. Similarly, all Germans must share in the responsibility for the crimes of the Nazis because they acquiesced with their silence. When we do not protest strongly against policies of our government we believe to be morally reprehensible, we too share in the guilt.

The Sodomites demanded, *"Bring them out to us that we may be intimate with them."*

> When pogrom-makers demand of Jews, "Hand over one of your number to us that we may kill him" or if they specify, "Hand over So and So that we may kill him; otherwise we shall kill all of you," it is better that all should die rather than hand over one person to be killed. And the same holds true when they demand the individual for sexual purposes (Midrash Or Ha'Afelah).

The dilemma that confronted Lot has unfortunately confronted Jews on many occasions when blood-thirsty mobs have demanded Jewish lives. Jewish law teaches that it is permissible to transgress almost all the commandments of Judaism in order to save one's life. There are, however, three exceptions—idolatry, murder and sexual immorality. In regard to murder, the Talmud tells us that if a man threatens, "I will kill you unless you kill so and so," it is forbidden to kill an innocent person even though your own life may be forfeited thereby. Self-defense is a sacred obligation but it is not permissible to cause the death of innocent third parties in order to save one's own life. Our own survival must not be purchased at the expense of that of our fellowmen.

To save his guests, Lot offered his two daughters to the Sodomites. *"You may do to them as you please, but do not do anything to these men."*

Lot behaved in much the same manner as the Sodomites. Ordinarily a man would be willing to die to protect his wife and daughters; he would kill or be killed. But Lot offers his own daughters to the Sodomites to do with as they wish (Tanchuma).

Unconsciously, Lot had adopted many of the attitudes of the Sodomites because of his closeness to them. Otherwise, he never would have made such an offer. Even when we think that we are uncontaminated by an evil environment, it can never be completely so. No matter how hard we may struggle against it, an unwholesome environment is bound to have some detrimental effect upon us.

The Sodomites refused to listen to the pleadings of Lot, replying instead, *"The fellow came here as an alien and already he acts the ruler!"*

They declared, "You have come to destroy laws established by previous generations" (Genesis Rabbah).

The assertion, "This is the way it has always been; therefore, this is the way it must be" is often used to justify the entrenchment of prejudice and injustice. Those who desire to change old-established laws or customs in the interest of justice and fair-play are regarded as dangerous subversives who are a menace to society.

Members of minority groups, in particular, often hesitate to speak out in defense of justice and morality because they are afraid that the charge hurled at Lot will be hurled at them. In our own country, unfortunately, many American Jews are intimidated from speaking out on behalf of social justice, because right-wing extremists and other anti-Semites denounce Jews as foreigners and aliens who seek to impose their viewpoint upon native-born Americans. It is time for all American Jews to recognize, however, that we render a disservice to America by remaining silent. We are not second-class citizens and have the right and the duty to speak out fearlessly against evils we see in American society.

When the Sodomites surged forward to break the door, the angels *pulled Lot into the house with them, and shut the door. And the people who were at the entrance of the house, young and old, they struck with blinding light.*

Notice that the young are here mentioned first in connection with the punishment. This is because they were the first to transgress, as it is written, *The men of Sodom, young and old, surrounded the house* (verse 4)—(Genesis Rabbah).

This is more than another illustration of "measure for measure." In Sodom, it was the young people who were in the forefront of the violence and immorality. In our society as well, the young people seem to be in the forefront of violence and immorality. The disruption of college and even high school education has become almost a commonplace occurrence. Inevitably, the ones who will suffer most from the disruption of the educational process, from the violence, from the lack of standards of morality and decency, will be the very same young people. Youth has the right and the duty to advocate change and to protest against what it considers to be unjust and immoral but it does not have

125

the right to resort to violence or to disrupt the education of others. Such tactics can only lead to repression and to the strengthening of the very totalitarian forces in society which the young people claim to oppose.

Fleeing the City

19:12-26

Even after being struck with blindness, the Sodomites continued to seek the door of Lot's house to do him violence. The angels then *said to Lot, "Whom else have you here."*

> What they meant was, "What else can you say in their defense? Until this point you had the right to try to defend them but now you no longer have that right" (Genesis Rabbah).

Abraham's and Lot's efforts to plead the cause of Sodom were admirable as long as there was something to be said in its defense. But when there is nothing more to be said in defense of the wicked, there comes a time for action, a time to destroy and eliminate the perpetrators of evil. Evil must be punished, and lovers of freedom do themselves and mankind a disservice when they continue to find excuses for the incorrigibly wicked in the name of "freedom of speech," or "the need for further discussion" or "the immaturity" of the individuals involved. If defenders of free speech and civil liberties allow themselves to be paralyzed into inaction or even actively plead the cause of those determined to destroy society, the result can only be the loss of freedom for all.

Finally realizing that the city was doomed, Lot urged his sons-in-law, *"Up, get out of this place for the Lord is about to destroy the city." But he seemed to his sons-in-law as one who jests.*

> They said to him, "Fool, harps and flutes are playing in the city, the city is filled with joy and laughter

and you claim that it will be destroyed" (Midrash HaGadol).

People who are prosperous are in no mood to take seriously prophecies of doom. The ruling classes immersed in revelry and luxury are usually taken totally by surprise when revolution brings their world crashing down upon their heads. Difficult indeed, therefore, is the lot of the individual who preaches to a prosperous community that the inevitable result of its corruption and immorality is destruction. The prophets of Israel had this most difficult and thankless task. Much more popular were the false prophets who proclaimed, " 'Peace, peace' when there is no peace" (Jeremiah 6:14). Our world and our nation today desperately need courageous leaders who, like the prophets of old, are not afraid to tell the people what they *should* hear instead of pursuing popularity by telling them what they *want* to hear.

The angels urged Lot to leave quickly, *"Lest you be swept away because of the iniquity of the city." Still he delayed.*

> From this we can learn that once the Destroyer has been unleashed, he does not differentiate between the righteous and the wicked (Sechel Tov).

War and destruction may be the inevitable consequences of wickedness but they do not consume only the wicked. Unfortunately, innocent people suffer along with the wicked in the ensuing devastation.

> Why did he delay? He kept on thinking, "What a loss of gold and silver and precious stones!" Lot thus was an illustration of the verse in Kohelet, "Riches kept by the owner thereof to his hurt" (5:12) — (Genesis Rabbah).

How many German Jews might have saved themselves during the early years of Hitler but did not leave Germany when they were able to get out because they could not take their wealth with them? Money can be a great blessing but it also can be the source of much harm to an individual when he places the preservation of his fortune above the well-being of himself and his family.

So the men seized his hand and brought him out of the city.

> When the angels first came to him as strangers, Lot took them by the hand and brought them into his home, even though they were at first unwilling. For this kindness, he merited being taken by the hand by the angels and brought outside the city even though he was unwilling (Pirkei d'Rabbi Eliezer).

One never knows in what manner a kindness extended will be repaid. Although the motive for extending a helping hand should not be the expectation of reward, nevertheless it generally turns out that kindness is repaid with kindness.

Lot was spared *in the Lord's mercy on him.*

> God had mercy on Lot and saved him because he had helped Abraham. When Abraham had gone into Egypt and had passed off his wife, Sarah, as his sister (12:13), Lot did not reveal his secret (Genesis Rabbah).

During the Nazi Occupation there were many Gentiles who knew the secret hiding places of Jews or who knew of Jews who were masquerading as non-Jews but did not reveal their secret. To this day we are grateful to those righteous Gentiles who aided Jews by keeping their secrets, if in no other way, and we pray that God spare them because they did not reveal the information that would have meant the death of innocent Jews.

Lot is told to flee to the mountain but he protests, *"I cannot escape to the mountain, lest disaster overtake me."*

> The mountain refers to Abraham who is called "mountain" in the Bible. In reality Lot was saying, "I cannot flee to Abraham because until now the Lord compared my deeds to those of my fellow citizens of Sodom and I was a righteous man compared

128

to them. But should I go to Abraham, whose good deeds far exceed mine, I shall be unable to survive" (Genesis Rabbah).

Lot may have been considered righteous when judged by the low standards of Sodom but could not possibly be considered righteous when judged by the high standards of Abraham. If we constantly seek to judge ourselves by the standards set by the finest and best individuals, we will never become too impressed with ourselves and our goodness. We should never be content to compare ourselves to those who are mediocre or worse, nor allow ourselves to take comfort in the thought, "but I'm not as bad as So and So."

After Lot had reached safety in Zoar, *the Lord rained upon Sodom and Gomorrah sulfurous fire from the Lord out of Heaven.*

Ordinarily the heavens are the source of mercy and blessing, as the Psalmist says, "Praise ye the Lord from the heavens" (148:1). Yet here the heavens are the source of destruction. This is to teach that God commanded the heavens from the very beginning, that they should do to man in accordance with man's actions. For the Sodomites the heavens produce sulphurous fire, for Israel they produce dew. Woe to the wicked, for they themselves cause that which should be a place of mercy to become for them a place of disaster (Tanchuma, Buber).

It is man who brings evil and destruction upon himself. Man is granted Free Will. If he uses it to do evil, then he brings destruction upon himself. In fact, the very things that should be a source of blessing are transformed into a curse. Witness atomic energy and all the great technological advances that have been made in modern times. These could be the source of unparalelled prosperity and blessing for mankind; instead, they pose the threat of total annihilation. It is man who determines whether the "heavens" are to be a source of blessing or a curse. "I call heaven and earth to

129

witness against you this day: I have put before you life and death, blessing and curse. Choose life" (Deut. 30:19).

Contrary to the instructions of the angels, Lot's wife *looked back and she thereupon turned into a pillar of salt.*

> Why of salt? She was punished by being turned into a pillar of salt because she had sinned with salt. She had refused to bring even a little salt to the table for her guests (cf. above, verse 3). According to another account, on the night that the angels visited Lot she went about to all her neighbors, saying to them, "Give me salt as we have guests." Her purpose was to make the people of the city aware of the presence of these outsiders. Therefore, she was *turned into a pillar of salt* (Genesis Rabbah).

The pillar of salt is thus but another instance of the wondrous ways of Divine Retribution. How often are people punished through the very instruments which they have used to hurt others!

> Another view holds that it was not idle curiosity that caused Lot's wife to look back but concern for her married daughters whom she had left behind in Sodom. She looked back hoping that they had decided to leave after all (Pirkei d'Rabbi Eliezer).

Concern for the members of one's family is only natural but when it leads a person to transgress the word of God, it can only lead to tragedy, as in the case of Lot's wife. She would have been better advised had she shown concern for their welfare when she still could have influenced them for good. There are parents who feel that for the sake of their children it is permissible to lie and cheat and do all sorts of immoral things. By so doing, however, they only bring disaster upon their children and upon themselves. Witness the parents who know their children are taking drugs and do everything to cover it up and to protect them from the authorities. They may feel they are helping their children but in reality they are destroying both their children and themselves. Parents should expend more effort seeking to influence their children to live decently, and less trying to help them avoid the consequences of their misdeeds.

Abraham Views the Destruction

19:27-29

Following the destruction of Sodom, Abraham got up early in the morning and *hurried to the place where he had stood before the Lord.*

> Standing before the Lord refers to prayer (The *Shemonah Esreh* prayer is known as the *Amidah*, the prayer that is recited standing.) From this verse we know that Abraham was the first one to introduce *Shachrit*, the Morning Prayer. In like manner, *Minchah*, the Afternoon Prayer, was instituted by Isaac and *Maariv*, the Evening Prayer, by Jacob (Berachot 26a).

To our Sages, it was inconceivable that there was ever a time that Jews did not pray regularly to God. Prayer is the natural expression of the religious feelings of man. Without prayer, life is rendered empty and meaningless. For the Jew, "life is fashioned by Prayer and prayer is the quintessence of life" (Heschel).

> Abraham *stood before the Lord* in prayer. From this we can learn that he who prays must feel that he is in the Presence of God (Sanhedrin 22a).

It is not enough to rattle off one's prayers in a perfunctory manner. When one prays, one must always be aware of "before Whom he stands." Prayer must be *Avodah She'blev*, "worship of the heart." *Kavonah*, proper intent and feeling, is essential if prayer is to be meaningful. "The worshipper must clear his mind of all private thoughts and regard himself as standing before the *Shechinah*, the Divine Presence," says Maimonides. One should pray with

131

feeling, "not like one who carrying a load, unloads it and leaves" (Yad, Tefillah 4:16). Would that every Jew who enters a synagogue to pray, would conduct himself as if he understood that he indeed *stood before the Lord.*

When He destroyed Sodom, God was mindful of Abraham and removed Lot from the midst of the upheaval.

God saved Lot because He was *mindful of Abraham*. Balaam, the Gentile prophet, said to Balak, King of Moab, "You are indeed guilty of ingratitude in seeking to destroy the Jews. If it were not for Abraham, their father, you would not even be in existence. Were it not for Abraham, Lot would not have been spared when Sodom was destroyed and you, as a Moabite, are a descendant of Lot" (Numbers Rabbah 20).

Can not the same charge of ingratitude be leveled with justice at Christianity? Were it not for Judaism there would have been no Christianity. Jesus was a Jew, all of his disciples were Jews and most of his teachings were Jewish in origin; yet, throughout the ages, Christianity has been guilty of the most vicious and unprovoked anti-Semitism.

The Daughters of Lot

19:30-38

And Lot went up out of Zoar and dwelt in the mountain.

Wherever you find the word *Vayeshev,* "and he dwelt," it means that trouble is not far off. Lot *dwelt* is followed by the disgraceful incident of his two daughters becoming pregnant by him while he was drunk. Jacob *dwelt* is followed by the heartache of the loss of Joseph (Midrash HaGadol, Vayeshev).

Whenever one just sits and relaxes, trouble is bound to follow, especially with children. Parents cannot take for granted that children will turn out well and therefore not expend time and effort on their moral development. "Sitting at ease" is an invitation to disaster. Parents must expend a great deal of effort and energy to insure that they will not have sorrow and heartbreak from their children.

Lot's daughters decide to become pregnant by their father.

> They did so because they thought that the entire world had been destroyed together with Sodom, and there would be no other way to repopulate the world. Had God judged them in accordance with the infamous act they committed, they would have deserved to be burned to death but God took into consideration their motive as well. Since their motive was the repopulation of the world, they were not punished as severely as they might otherwise have been (Midrash HaGadol).

Even a worthy motive does not excuse an unworthy act. Nevertheless, we should take into account what brought about a particular act before affixing blame and punishment. "Never judge your neighbor until you are in his place," say our Sages. Sometimes, there are extenuating circumstances which, while not justifying the unworthy action, at least make it understandable.

The older one went in and lay with her father.

> "Throw a stick into the air, it falls back whence it came." The older daughter was the first to commit the immoral act and it was her descendants who were the first to be guilty of immoral acts. She was the mother of Moab, and of the daughters of Moab in the wilderness we are told, *The people began to commit harlotry with the daughters of Moab* (Numbers 25:1) — (Tanchuma, Buber, Balak 26).

"The apple does not fall far from the tree." Children emulate the actions of their parents. The Torah is correct when it says that "the sins of the fathers are visited upon the children," not because children are punished for sins they did not commit but because children tend to behave like their parents.

Lot *did not know when she lay down or when she rose.*

> In the Masoretic text there is a dot over one of the letters in the Hebrew word meaning *when she rose.* This is to indicate that although Lot did not know *when she lay down* with him because he was drunk, he was aware of *when she rose.* But even if he knew then, what difference did it make? What was done was done! Nevertheless, he should have at least learned not to drink wine the next time (Nazir 23a).

It is one thing to make a mistake once, but to make the same mistake a second time is inexcusable. A fool is one who does not learn from his mistakes. A great deal of the war and misery in the world is caused by the unwillingness or inability of leaders to learn from past mistakes. It is true that there is no point in "crying over spilt milk" but we can at least be careful not to spill it again and again.

Thus the two daughters of Lot came to be with child by their father. The older one bore a son and named him Moab . . . the younger also bore a son, and she called him Ben-Ammi.

> Because the older one disgraced her father publicly by calling her child Moab which means "by my father," her descendants, the Moabites, were punished in that Israel was permitted to divert their rivers and burn their homes. The younger daughter, however, spared her father's honor, calling her child Ben Ammi, meaning "son of one who was with me (*Immi*), without specifying who that one was. Therefore, her descendants, the Ammonites, were spared; Israel being told not to contend with them in any manner whatsoever (Genesis Rabbah).

Sparing the feelings of a person, and not holding him up to disgrace and ridicule, is a most important principle of

Judaism. Tamar, the daughter-in-law of Judah, did not publicly embarrass him even though she was about to be burned for adultery. Instead she declared, "I am with child by the man to whom these belong" (Gen. 38:25). Our Sages go so far as to declare that "he who humiliates his fellow-man in public is as if he has shed his blood" (Baba Metzia 58b).

The sparing of the Ammonites because their ancestress used the circumlocution "son of one who was with me" indicates that God rewards even for pure speech (Baba Kamma 38b).

In this day and age when there is so much obscenity and the use of four-letter words is commonplace, it is well to keep in mind the virtue of clean speech. The kind of language we use will affect not only the kind of language our children will use but their moral values as well.

CHAPTER 10

Sarah in the House of Abimelech

20:1-7

And Abraham journeyed from there to the region of the Negeb.

Why? Because once Sodom had been destroyed, wayfarers ceased in the area and Abraham said, "Shall I permit hospitality to cease from my house?" Therefore he went and pitched his tent in Gerar (Genesis Rabbah).

Abraham would not permit himself to live in a community where the opportunity to serve his fellowman was limited. A truly righteous individual not only does not shirk opportunities for service when they present themselves, but is actually unhappy when such opportunities do not exist and does not want to live in such a community.

Another reason for Abraham's leaving was to get away from Lot who had besmirched the family reputation. People were saying, "Lot, Abraham's nephew, had sexual relations with his two daughters" (Genesis Rabbah).

Lot's behavior reflected adversely upon Abraham and the entire family. A person's reputation is not just "his own business." It affects the lives and the reputations of all the members of his family.

While he was sojourning in Gerar, Abraham said of Sarah his wife, "She is my sister." So Abimelech king of Gerar had Sarah brought to him. But God came to Abimelech in a dream by night.

What is the difference between the prophets of Israel and those of other nations? One difference is that God appears to the Gentile prophets only at night. He appeared to Balaam at night (Numbers 22:20), to Laban at night (Gen. 31:24) and *to Abimelech in a dream by night* (Genesis Rabbah).

God speaks to and through individuals of all nations, but the message of God came most directly to, and was articulated most effectively by, the prophets of Israel. Other nations have produced prophets but only the teachings enunciated by the prophets of Israel have withstood the light of day. Only their prophetic message has had a profound impact upon the conscience and moral development of mankind.

And said to him, "You are to die because of the woman that you have taken, for she is a married woman." Abimelech, however, protested, *"Oh Lord, will You slay people even though innocent? . . . When I did this my heart was blameless and my hands were clean."*

Abimelech's defense was, "Master of the Universe, You know that which is hidden and that which is revealed but *I* did not know that she was a married woman" (Pesikta Rabbati 42).

Although Abimelech is by no means completely blameless, his claim that he should not be punished for what he contemplated doing out of ignorance is accepted by God. Judaism does make a distinction between sins committed unwittingly and sins committed wilfully as an outright act of rebellion against God's moral law.

God answers, *"I knew that you did this with a blameless heart."*

Said God to him, "In one respect you speak truthfully, in another you speak falsely. When you say, *'My heart was blameless,'* you speak truthfully. However, when you maintain, *'My hands were clean,'* you speak falsely." That is why here God mentions only *a blameless heart* but does not mention the "clean hands" that Abimelech had referred to (Tanchuma, Buber).

Abimelech's heart may have been blameless in that he did not originally think of sinning. But his hands were not clean because when the opportunity presented itself he wanted to sin. A person who has not sinned simply because the opportunity has not presented itself is not deserving of moral praise for should the opportunity present itself, he, like Abimelech, may not possess the moral fortitude to resist temptation. Only the individual who has the strength of character to resist sinning when the opportunity is at hand is deserving of our approbation. "Who is mighty? He who subdues his evil impulse" (Avot 4:1).

"I kept you from sinning against Me. That was why I did not let you touch her."

> It is like the case of a warrior who was riding his horse at full speed when, seeing a child lying in the path, he reined in the horse so that the child was not hurt. Who deserves the praise, the horse or the rider? Surely, the rider! Similarly here, the praise belongs to God not to Abimelech, for it was God who prevented Abimelech from sinning (Genesis Rabbah).

Abimelech refrained from forcing his attentions upon Sarah not because he was a man of conscience and morality but because God prevented him from doing so by rendering him impotent. Sometimes, when a person who has every desire and inclination to commit an illegal or immoral act is prevented from doing so by circumstances beyond his control, he turns around and wraps himself in a mantle of righteousness. Loudly he proclaims his own virtue, as did Abimelech, while denouncing others, more successful than he, for their immoral behavior.

"But you must restore the man's wife—since he is a prophet, he will intercede for you—to save your life."

> What does this mean? That a *prophet's* wife must be restored but an ordinary person's wife does not

have to be restored? Of course not! What is meant is that "You, Abimelech, cannot plead innocence on the grounds that Abraham claimed that his wife was his sister. *He is a prophet* and from your question he knew what he had to answer." When a traveller comes to a city, he is usually asked about food and lodging, not "Is this your wife or your sister?" (Makkot 9b).

When Abraham heard such a question being asked, he realized his life was in danger and therefore he answered that she was his sister. Abraham may not have been blameless in trying to pass off Sarah as his sister, but the fact that he felt constrained to do so is a damning indictment of the society of Gerar where a man could not feel safe with his own wife. One can learn a great deal about the character of a particular society or community from the lies and subterfuges people feel compelled to resort to in order to survive.

A man who has paid compensation for an injury he has caused is nevertheless not forgiven until he has asked the injured party's forgiveness. We know this from the fact that God tells Abimelech not only, *"Restore the man's wife"* but *"he will intercede for you."* You must ask his forgiveness and thus gain his goodwill to the point where he will be willing to intercede for you (Baba Kamma 92a).

Paying reparations is not enough. An individual or a nation that has committed a grievous wrong must not think that simply by writing a check the wrong has been righted and the obligation fulfilled. In addition, the guilty party must do everything possible, both in word and in deed, to prove that he is truly penitent and sincerely asks forgiveness, to the point where the aggrieved party will be willing to intercede in his behalf.

Abimelech Confronts Abraham

20:8-18

Abimelech summoned Abraham and said to him, "What have you done to us? What wrong have I done you that you should bring so great a guilt upon me and my kingdom?"

> Abimelech mentions guilt brought upon his kingdom because a ruler is to his country what the heart is to a man. When the heart takes sick, the entire body is sick. Similarly, when a ruler sins it is the sin of the entire country, and the entire country becomes deserving of destruction (Midrash HaGadol).

A nation cannot excuse its actions by placing the blame on its ruler; the entire country must share in the guilt. After the Second World War, many Germans sought to place all the blame for the Nazi War Crimes upon Hitler, claiming ignorance or helplessness on their part. Every German, however, whether an active Nazi or not, must bear some measure of guilt for without the participation and acquiescence of the German people Hitler could never have risen to power, nor carried out his diabolical scheme of extermination.

> The fact that Abimelech refers to *so great a guilt* shows that sexual immorality is a more serious sin than almost anything else. How much more so when it involves a married woman! (Midrash HaGadol).

Sexual immorality, particularly among married couples, is a most serious matter and should not be treated lightly as is so often the case in our permissive society. Such immorality undermines not only the sanctity of marriage but the very foundations of family life and of our entire civilization.

Abraham defends his actions by declaring to Abimelech, *"I thought surely there is no fear of God in this place, and they will kill me because of my wife."*

The fear of God is of great importance, for when one is a God-fearing person it can be assumed that he will refrain from sinning; but when a person is not God-fearing it can be assumed that he will not hold back from committing a sin (Midrash Ha-Gadol).

There are those who maintain that ethical living need not be rooted in belief in God and religion. However, it is undoubtedly true that belief in God and acceptance of religious values provide indispensable support for ethical living and that the ethical values even of those who claim to be non-religious are rooted in the teachings of religion. It was in his Farewell Address that George Washington warned his fellow citizens, "Let us with caution indulge the supposition that morality can be maintained without religion."

Abimelech restored Sarah to Abraham and urged him to remain in Gerar. *"Here, my land is before you; settle wherever you please."*

Abimelech thus showed himself to be a pious Gentile who wanted to be the neighbor of a righteous man (Pesikta Zutrati).

It is a wise person who recognizes the need to live in proximity to decent, righteous individuals. Neighbors who are good people have a beneficial effect upon all the members of the family; while neighbors who are undesirable can be a very bad influence upon members of the family, especially the young and impressionable ones. How many youngsters have gotten into trouble because they associated with the type of neighbors who were an undesirable influence! The advice of Pirkei Avot is sage advice indeed, "Keep yourself far from a bad neighbor" (1:7) ; "Go forth and see which is the good way to which a man should cleave. . . . Rabbi Jose said: 'A good neighbor' " (2:13).

Abraham then prayed to God.

Let every man learn proper behavior from our Father Abraham. Was there anyone more deeply wronged than he? Yet once Abimelech asked forgiveness of him, he forgave with a complete heart and not only did he forgive but he prayed to God on his behalf (Midrash HaGadol).

It is forbidden to bear a grudge. The Torah proclaims, "Thou shalt not take vengeance nor bear any grudge against the children of thy people, but thou shalt love thy neighbor as thyself: I am the Lord" (Lev. 19:18). From the fact that after Abimelech asked his forgiveness Abraham not only forgave him but prayed to God on his behalf, we learn that if the one wronged refuses to forgive he is considered cruel (Baba Kamma 92a). The Testament of the Twelve Patriarchs goes even further. "If a man sin against thee, cast forth the poison of hate and speak peaceably to him. If he confess and repent, forgive him. But if he be shameless and persist in his wrongdoing, even so forgive him from the heart, and leave to God the avenging."

Abraham's praying to God on behalf of Abimelech is the first instance in the Bible of anyone praying on behalf of someone else (Genesis Rabbah).

It is one thing to pray to God for one's self; it is far more meritorious to pray on behalf of the welfare and well-being of another human being.

And God healed Abimelech, his wife and his slave girls, so that they bore children.

Abraham's prayer was answered so that *they bore children* even though they had been barren previously (Pesikta Rabbati).

When one prays on behalf of another with no thought of personal profit, his prayer is far more likely to be answered than if he prays for himself.

Abraham prayed on behalf of Abimelech and his wife that they not be barren and God answered his prayer on their behalf. Said the angels to God, "Master of the Universe, Abraham brings healing to others, yet he is in need of the same healing himself.

142

Will you not heal him?" Said God, "He is indeed worthy that I should give him children" (Tanchuma, Buber).

We read of the birth of a son to Abraham and Sarah immediately after we read of Abraham's prayer on behalf of Abimelech and his wife that they should bear children. When one prays on behalf of another, it is more likely that God will answer his prayers on his own behalf as well. God blesses the individual who is not so self-centered as to think only of himself but is concerned about the welfare of others.

CHAPTER 11

Birth of Isaac

21:1-8

The Lord took note of Sarah as He had promised.

It was on Rosh Hashanah that God *took note of Sarah* so that she conceived and bore a son. Rachel and Hannah, also, were remembered by God on Rosh Hashanah so that they bore sons (Rosh Hashanah 11a).

We are told that God determined upon the birth of Isaac, Joseph and the prophet Samuel on Rosh Hashanah. Rosh Hashanah is the "birthday of the world" but it is the birth of righteous individuals that alone makes the creation of the world significant and worthwhile for without righteous human beings the world could not long survive.

Connecting *Pakad, took note,* with *Pikadon,* a deposit, the Sages comment that God is a trustee who returns what is deposited with Him. Amalek deposited with Him bundles of thorns (evil deeds); therefore, God returned to him bundles of thorns (punishment) as it says, *"I remember (Pakadti) that which Amalek did to Israel* (ISam. 15:2). Sarah deposited with him bundles of roses, i.e. a store of pious acts and good deeds; therefore, God returned to her a son Isaac, as a reward for her pious acts and good deeds (Genesis Rabbah).

Wickedness is punished; righteousness is rewarded. It may not always *seem* to be so but ultimately it *is* so. You get out of life what you put into it. Sarah put good deeds and righteous living into the development of her son Isaac and she got out of him what she put in. Parents who bemoan the moral character of their children may well ask themselves, "What did we put into our children?"

God is not like those who speak but do not perform. He had made a promise, *"Sarah shall have a son"* (18:14) and He fulfilled His promise (Genesis Rabbah).

It was Balaam, the Gentile prophet, who declared, "God is not man to be capricious or mortal to change His mind. Would He speak and not act—promise and not fulfill?" (Numbers 23:19). Throughout centuries of persecution and oppression Jews took comfort in the fact that the word of God could be relied upon. God had promised that He would not utterly destroy His people but would redeem them and bring them back to their own land and surely He would keep that promise. In our day, we have been privileged to witness the fulfillment of God's promise to His people through His prophets.

It is also possible to understand the verse to mean that "the Lord took note of Sarah as *Abraham* had said (to Abimelech)." Abraham had prayed on behalf of Abimelech that he might have children (20:17) ; therefore, *the Lord took note of Sarah.* The verse would thus be the source of the Rabbinic statement, "Whoever asks on behalf of his fellow and is in need of the same thing himself, is answered first" (Baba Kamma 92a).

As long as you have compassion upon your fellow, God has compassion upon you. Abraham prayed on behalf of Abimelech and immediately received his own reward in that Sarah conceived and bore him a son (Tanchuma, Buber).

God had compassion upon Abraham because Abraham had compassion upon Abimelech. On the High Holy Days we come to the Synagogue to ask God to have compassion upon us. However, we have no right to expect God to have compassion upon us unless we have compassion upon our fellow human beings and pray and work for their well-being and welfare, as well as for our own.

And the Lord did (Va'ya'as) for Sarah as He had spoken.

The word *Va'ya'as* is also used in reference to the creation of the lights in the heavens: *God made (Va'ya'as) the two great lights* (Genesis 1:16). Just as there the purpose was to give light to the world, so, here, too, the purpose of the birth of Isaac was to give light to the world (Pesikta d'Rabbi Kahana 2).

It was through Isaac and his descendants that the light of truth, morality and religion was disseminated to the world, for without Isaac, Abraham's teachings would have died with him and been lost to the world. The Jew has always been "a light unto the nations" spreading the highest ethical and moral values of religion to the darkest corners of the human heart and mind.

Abraham gave his new-born son, whom Sarah had borne him, the name of Isaac (Yitzchak).

The name signifies "Law has gone forth" (Yatza Chok) to the world; a gift has been given to the world (Genesis Rabbah).

One of the great contributions of Judaism to the world is the emphasis upon Law. The Religion of Love of Christianity is frequently contrasted with the Religion of Law of Judaism, to the disparagement of Judaism. While Judaism has never ignored Love—Love of God and of one's fellowman—we do not deny or apologize for the fact that Judaism is a Religion of Law. We maintain that only through Law can the abstract doctrine of Love be made concrete. The giving to the world of the concept of Law is indeed one of Judaism's great gifts to mankind.

Sarah said, "God has brought me joy; everyone who hears will rejoice with me."

Why would the birth of a son to Sarah be a cause of rejoicing to others? It was because many other barren women were remembered with her; many deaf gained their hearing, many blind had their eyes opened, many who were insane became sane (Genesis Rabbah).

Many others benefitted from Sarah's good fortune. Indeed, thus it has always been; the good fortune of the Jews has been a source of blessing not only to himself but to the entire community and country in which he lived. Those countries that permitted Jews to live freely and to participate in the economic, cultural and social life of the nation found that the entire nation benefitted immeasurably. If only the Arab nations today would permit Israel to live in peace, they, too, would soon find the Jewish State to be a source of blessing and benefit to Arab as well as Jew.

Ishmael's Immorality

21:9-10

As her son Isaac grew up, *Sarah saw the son, whom Hagar the Egyptian had borne to Abraham, playing* (*Me'tsachek*) and demanded that Abraham banish the boy Ishmael and his mother.

> The word *Me'tsachek,* "*playing,*" refers to immorality, idolatry and bloodshed (Genesis Rabbah).
> "Banish him lest my son learn his ways," she demanded (Exodus Rabbah 1).

Sarah's demand that Ishmael be banished was not due to jealousy or caprice. She was concerned lest her son learn from Ishmael's bad example. Parents should be concerned about the type of children their own children associate with. It is most important for youngsters to associate with others who are fine and decent young people. How many youngsters go astray simply because they "pal around" with the wrong element and thus get into trouble themselves.

Had not Sarah seen Ishmael *"playing"* in this

147

manner before? After all, he had been acting in this manner all his young life. Why then did she not seek to have him banished before this? (Midrash HaBiur).

Sarah had been perturbed by Ishmael's actions even before Isaac was born but it was only after Isaac's birth that she found the situation intolerable. She was moved to action only because of the threat that Ishmael's behavior posed to the moral development, and perhaps even to the physical survival, of her own son, Isaac. Unfortunately, people are usually not stirred to action by injustice until they are directly involved.

What about Abraham? Did he not see the immoral behavior of his son, Ishmael? In this instance, Abraham was the epitome of the truth expressed by the verse in Proverbs, "He who spares the rod spoils the child." Abraham could not bring himself to discipline and chastise his son, Ishmael. As a result, Ishmael went astray and eventually had to be banished from his father's house (Exodus Rabbah 1).

The parent who truly loves his child will not hesitate to discipline him. Parents who cannot, or will not, discipline their children run the grave risk of losing them completely. True love is demonstrated not by permissiveness but by firmness.

Abraham exemplifies the verse, "and shutteth his eyes from looking upon evil" (Isaiah 33:15) — (Genesis Rabbah).

Abraham shut his eyes to what Ishmael was doing. He didn't see because he did not want to see. Parents often seem to be the last to know when their children get into trouble. The danger signals are there for all to see but the parents do not see because they do not want to come to grips with the reality of the situation; they try to delude themselves into believing that all is well. The result for Abraham was disastrous and so it is for any parent "who shuts his eyes."

Playing. Ishmael would go out into the fields with Isaac and shoot arrows at him, claiming innocently,

"But I am only playing" (Tosefta Sotah 6; cf. Rashi here).

Some parents tend to ignore the malicious or disagreeable actions of their children, rationalizing that "they are still young" or "they are only playing." However, one can learn a great deal about a child's character from the way he plays and parents would be well-advised to pay more attention to the play habits of their children.

Notice, also, that a bow and arrow was one of Ishmael's first toys so that from his earliest childhood he learned to "play" at making war and at killing. We should be very careful about the kind of toys we permit our children to play with. Guns and tanks, toy soldiers and games glorifying war and violence should not be encouraged as playthings lest they help to produce a generation that accepts war and violence as an integral and acceptable part of daily living.

The Banishment

21:11-21

Abraham is very distressed at Sarah's demand but God tells him, *"Whatever Sarah tells you, do as she says."*

From this we learn that Abraham was secondary to Sarah when it came to prophecy (Exodus Rabbah 1).

God said to Abraham, "Sarah is your companion, the wife of your youth. Whatever she has said is the truth; therefore, *do as she says"* (Pirkei d'Rabbi Eliezer).

Judaism is often accused of according very low status to the woman. Nothing could be further from the truth. Although she did not possess "equal rights" in the modern sense, the Jewish wife was placed upon a pedestal and the Jewish husband invariably followed her advice and counsel.

God reassures Abraham, *"It is through Isaac that offspring shall be continued for you. As for the son of the slave-woman, I will make a nation of him, too, for he is your seed."*

> Ishmael is referred to here not as the "son of Abraham" but as *the son of the slave woman.* From this we learn that only a son born of a Jewish mother is called "your son" but a son born of a Jewish father and a non-Jewish mother is not called "your son" but "her son" (Pesikta Zutrati, Pinchas 132).

Jewish descent is from the mother. The child of a Jewish mother is Jewish even if the father is not; the child of a non-Jewish mother is not Jewish even if the father is. Young men contemplating marrying out of the faith are often unaware of this fact and are under the mistaken impression that their children will be Jewish just because they want them to be. They should realize that if they marry out of the faith their children will not be Jewish but will automatically acquire the faith of their mother.

Abraham sent her away and she strayed in the wilderness of Beer-sheba.

> This means that she strayed after other Gods. As soon as she left the jurisdiction of Abraham she reverted back to the idolatry that she had known in her father's house (Pirkei d'Rabbi Eliezer 30).

Judaism does not eagerly embrace those who seek to convert only in order to marry a Jewish partner because frequently such a conversion is only superficial, a "conversion of convenience" rather than a total transformation. There is the danger that at the first sign of trouble in the marriage, the convert will revert back to his or her original beliefs and that the conversion to Judaism will have little or no lasting impact upon the faith, attitudes and practices of the individual. Of course, this is not always the case. There are many who become sincerely attached to their new faith and remain loyal to it no matter what the hardships; witness Ruth, the Moabite girl who became the ancestress of King David.

When the water was gone . . . she left the child under one
of the bushes and went and sat down at a distance, a bow-
shot away (Ki'mi'tachavey Keshet).

Through a play on words, the Rabbis connect
Ki'mi'tachavey with *Ki'ma'te'chet* (as one who criti-
cizes). Hagar was as one who criticized God, complaining, "Yesterday You promised me, *I will greatly*
increase your offspring (Gen. 16:10) and now he is
dying of thirst" (Genesis Rabbah).

It is interesting that it is precisely the one who denies
God and the Law of God who is most bitter at God when
suffering and tragedy come. The individual who serves God
faithfully all his life is most likely, when trouble comes, to
accept it without complaint; declaring, "Shall we receive
good at the hand of God, and shall we not receive evil?"
(Job 2:10). It is the person who has ignored God all his
life who is most likely to berate God and to complain, "Why
did God do this to me?"

Sitting thus afar, she burst into tears. God heard the cry
of the boy.

Hagar was the one who *burst into tears;* yet we
are told, *God heard the cry of the boy.* From this we
can learn that a sick person's prayer on his own
behalf is sooner answered by God than another's
prayer on his behalf (Genesis Rabbah).

Frequently, a Rabbi will be asked by a person who is ill
or in distress, "Rabbi, pray for me." Judaism does not believe in vicarious prayer or in Prayer by Proxy. The prayer
of a Rabbi in behalf of an individual is not only not more
efficacious but even less so, than that individual's sincere
prayer on his own behalf. Every person, no matter what
his station in life or his level of education, is expected by
Judaism to approach God directly and not through any
emissary or agent. The Rabbi can teach, can guide, can
inspire a person to pray but he cannot "pray for him."

And an angel of God called to Hagar from heaven and said

*to her, "What troubles you, Hagar? Fear not, for God has
heeded the cry of the boy where he is."*

What is the meaning of the phrase *where he is?*
It means *where he is* morally at the present moment.
A man is judged only according to his present actions and not according to the evil deeds that he
may commit at some future time. The angels accused Ishmael before God, pointing to the cruelty
that his descendants would display towards the Jewish people in the future. Said God to them, "What
is he now?" When they had to admit that at the
present moment he was righteous, God declared, "I
judge man only as he is at the moment" (Genesis
Rabbah).

A person should not be punished for crimes or sins that
it is believed he may commit in the future. God, to whom
knowledge of the future is a foreknown certainty, nevertheless refused to punish on the basis of what would be in
the future. Certainly, therefore, we who do not possess such
certainty must refrain from punishing or condemning on
the basis of what we believe a man may do at some future
time. We can judge a man only on the basis of what he has
done and not on the basis of what we think he may do.

Then God opened her eyes and she saw a well of water.

All may be presumed to be blind until God en-
lightens their eyes (Genesis Rabbah).

The well of water was there all the time but Hagar did
not see it until *God opened her eyes.* We are surrounded by
"wells of water," by blessings of all sorts, but our eyes do
not see and our hearts do not appreciate until God opens
our eyes and our hearts. Far too often blessings go un-
noticed and unappreciated even though they are close at
hand. It is not only idols who "have eyes but they see not"
(Ps. 115:5) ; it is true of human beings as well.

God provided a well of water for Hagar. When
Moses in the wilderness showed lack of faith in God's

152

ability to provide water for the Children of Israel, God said to him, "You should have learned from the experience of Hagar. If I raised up a well of water for one individual, Ishmael, whose only merit was his father Abraham, how much more so would I provide water for Israel who have not only the merit of the Patriarchs, but also the merit of the Torah which they received and the merit of the commandments (Yalkut Shimoni I 764).

We must learn to have faith in God's ability and willingness to provide. An individual who lives a righteous, God-fearing life should look forward with hope and confidence to the providence of the Almighty.

Ishmael survived and *became a bowman.*

> He would take a bow and arrows and would shoot at birds (Pirkei d'Rabbi Eliezer 30).

It was a mark of Ishmael's cruelty and insensitivity to the suffering of others that he could derive pleasure from the senseless shooting of a bird or animal. The Rabbis regarded with abhorrence those who would make out of the killing of living creatures a sport. It is one thing to slaughter an animal or bird for the benefit of man; it is a totally different thing to kill for the pleasure of killing. Judaism has always looked with disfavor upon the hunter and the so-called sport of hunting.

And his mother got a wife for him from the land of Egypt.

> Hagar herself came from Egypt (16:1) and when it came time to find a wife for Ishmael she turned to the land of Egypt. As the saying goes, "Throw a stick into the air, and it will come back to its place of origin" (Genesis Rabbah).

It is most difficult to free oneself completely from one's background. Despite all her years in the household of Abraham, in the moment of decision Hagar still regarded herself as an Egyptian. In and of itself this attraction to one's own roots is a good thing but it should be borne in mind by those who, contemplating intermarriage, feel that all problems can be solved through conversion. A non-Jew, even with the best of intentions, will find it extremely difficult to divest himself of his background, just as would a Jew contemplating converting out of his faith for the sake of marriage.

A Treaty of Peace

21:22-34

At that time Abimelech and Phichol, chief of his troops, said to Abraham, "God is with you in everything you do."

What brought Abimelech to the realization that God was with Abraham? Previously, the people of the world had thought, "Were he a righteous man, would he not have been blessed with children?" Therefore, when he did have a child, they said to him, "God is with you" (Genesis Rabbah).

People tend to judge others on the basis of tangible things, for this is all they can see. They regard material blessings as proof of God's favor and, conversely, the lack of such blessings as an indication of God's disfavor. Although God does reward the righteous and punish the wicked, it is unfair for us to judge others on the basis of the blessings that have been given or withheld from them because it is not given to us to be able to fathom God's purposes.

"Therefore swear to me here by God that you will not deal falsely with me, or with my son, or with my son's son" . . . *and Abraham said, "I will swear."*

What was the reason that when the Children of Israel left Egypt and began their sojourn towards the Promised Land *God did not lead them by way*

of the land of the Philistines, although it was nearer?
(Exodus 13:17). It was because Abimelech's grandson was still alive at the time (Genesis Rabbah).

God remembered the oath made by Abraham to Abimelech and protected his grandson under the terms of the oath. A solemn promise must be kept even if it is inconvenient to do so. The Third Commandment, "You shall not swear falsely by the name of the Lord your God," warns against breaking a promise or agreement which has been sealed with an oath.

> Notice, the text does not say "And Abraham swore" as one would expect, but *I will swear*. The fact that Abraham said, "I *will* swear" was enough. From this you can learn that once a person has agreed to swear, it is as if he had already sworn, even though he has not yet done so. From this you can also see that the words of a Jew are as an oath (Midrash Habiur).

It is not necessary to formally take an oath in order to be bound by what one has said. In fact, Jewish tradition opposes the use of oaths entirely. We are admonished that even without swearing, "Let your 'yes' be true and your 'no' be true" (Baba Metzia 46a). In the light of this, it is ironic that, using the Kol Nidre as their proof, anti-Semites often allege that a Jew's word cannot be relied upon. Of course, the Kol Nidre refers only to nullifying oaths "between man and God," not to oaths between "man and man." Even more, however, far from showing that a Jew's word cannot be relied upon, the solemnity surrounding the Kol Nidre indicates the importance the Jew attaches to an oath and even to a promise made without an oath.

Then Abraham reproached Abimelech for the well of water which the servants of Abimelech had seized.

> Following Abraham's reproach to Abimelech, a treaty of peace was made between them. From this we can see that reproach leads to peace and that peace unaccompanied by reproach is not peace (Genesis Rabbah).

155

It is interesting that the first recorded peace treaty in history was agreed upon only after Abraham severely rebuked Abimelech for the injustices committed by his servants. Peace cannot be achieved by appeasement, by closing one's eyes to injustice and pretending it does not exist. Chamberlain, at Munich, made the mistake of thinking that appeasement could bring peace; to his sorrow and, more importantly, to the sorrow of mankind, he found that it could not. Peace among nations can be achieved only when grievances are brought into the open and settled. Otherwise, they become festering sores that make true peace impossible.

What is true of nations is true also of individuals. In order for there to be peace and love between husband and wife, between parents and children, between partners or between neighbors, there must be a willingness to reprove and rebuke openly, when necessary. If a slight, real or fancied, is not brought into the open but is harbored in silent resentment, it will fester and grow until it threatens the entire relationship. From Abraham we should learn to bring all resentments into the open and resolve them, so that true peace and understanding can be established.

After they had concluded the pact of peace at Beersheba, Abimelech departed and Abraham *planted a tamarisk (Eshel) at Beer-sheba and invoked there the name of the Lord, the Everlasting God.*

> What is the meaning of the word *Eshel*. One Sage says it means he planted an orchard so that he could provide food for all. Another says it means he established an inn to provide for the needs of wayfarers. A third Sage maintains it means that he established a court of law (Genesis Rabbah).

If we are to create a peaceful and happy world, then like Abraham we must be concerned with these three things. We must see to it that none starve or go hungry anywhere in the world. Secondly, we must make certain that there are none who go homeless; that every human being has a decent place to live. Finally, we must establish the rule of law in the world for individuals and for nations so that every human being will feel that he is being treated with justice and with dignity. Only thus can there be a true pact of peace among nations and within nations.

According to the view that it was an inn, Abraham would provide hospitality to wayfarers and after they had partaken of his hospitality he would say to them, "Now say Grace." When they would ask what they should say, he would reply, "Blessed be the Everlasting God, of whose bounty we have partaken." That is why it says that he *invoked there the name of the Lord, the Everlasting God* (Genesis Rabbah).

Abraham wasted no opportunity to bring people to an appreciation of the God of Israel. Whatever he did, he saw as an opportunity to sanctify the Name of God. We too should be alert to every opportunity to sanctify the name of God and to bring credit upon the name of Israel.

CHAPTER 12

God Tests Abraham

22:1-2

Some time afterward God put Abraham to the test.

> Test followed test and greatness followed greatness (Genesis Rabbah).

The *Akedah* was not a punishment from God, it was a test. It was a test of Abraham's character; not for God to find out about Abraham but for Abraham to find out about himself and for others to become aware of him. Out of this and other tests there emerged the greatness of the man.

> Through a play on words, *Nisah,* "put to the test," is connected with *Nes,* "a ship's banner." God tests the righteous in order that he may exalt them in the world like a ship's banner flying aloft (Genesis Rabbah).

Just as the sea-worthiness of a ship cannot be tested as it lies at rest in the harbor, but only on the high seas amidst the waves and the breakers, so the worthiness of a human being cannot be tested when he dwells in peace and tranquility but only amidst the storms and stresses of life. Through God's testing, Abraham discovered that he could face trouble and conquer it, proudly holding aloft his banner of faith. Like Abraham we must learn to meet adversity squarely, without faltering or "striking our colors," and to emerge from our trials stronger in faith and in character.

> God puts the righteous to the test before exalting them like a ship's banner in order that His justice may be verified in the world and it may become apparent to all that God does not enrich or impoverish

arbitrarily. Should a person say to you that God gave Abraham wealth and power arbitrarily and without justification, you can answer him, "Can you do what Abraham did in being willing to offer his son as a sacrifice after the pain of being childless so long?" (Genesis Rabbah).

God's blessings are not bestowed arbitrarily and without justification. Usually, a man who has been blessed with success has earned that success through hard work and much sacrifice. It is the failure in life who is always attributing the success of others to luck. Success and greatness generally come only to those who have been able to stand the test and prove their mettle under the most trying circumstances.

It is only the righteous who are put to the test. A potter does not test defective vessels by striking them, because even a single blow will break them. What type of vessel does he test? Only sound vessels, for even many blows will not break them. Similarly, God tests not the wicked but the righteous, as it says, "The Lord trieth the righteous" (Ps. 11:5). When a man possess two cows, one strong and the other feeble, upon which does he place the yoke? Upon the strong one, of course. In the same way, God tests only the righteous (Genesis Rabbah).

When a person undergoes all sorts of trial and ordeals, we have no right to assume that they are a sign of divine displeasure, punishment for sins committed. On the contrary, "The Lord trieth the righteous," for it is only they who have the moral fortitude and spiritual stamina to withstand such trials. The Book of Job teaches this lesson; that although we may attribute our *own* suffering to our sins, we have no right to attribute the suffering and sorrow of others to sins they must have committed.

God called to Abraham *and he answered, Here I am (Hi'ne'ni).*

Here I am (*Hi'ne'ni*) connotes humility and saintliness (Tanchuma).

It is interesting that our Sages associated coming forward and declaring, *"Hi'ne'ni,* Here I am, ready to serve" with humility and saintliness. When called upon to serve a worthy cause, it is false humility to say, "Who am I? Why call upon me? I am not worthy." The truly humble person while recognizing his own shortcomings and failings, does not use them as a pretext for shirking responsibility. Far from being a sign of conceit or arrogance, coming forward and saying, *"Hi'ne'ni,* Here I am, I will accept the responsibility because it is a sacred obligation and someone must undertake it," is a manifestation of true humility and saintliness.

> Because Abraham answered *Hi'ne'ni* God promised him, "I will bestow reward upon your children with the very same expression." Thus it is written, *Behold (Hi'ne'ni) I will rain down bread for you from the sky* (Exodus 16:4)—(Exodus Rabbah 25).

Abraham's willingness to serve God led to blessing for his children. When we serve worthy causes, our example has a profound impact upon our children. By so doing, we inspire them to devote themselves to noble endeavors and thus to be worthy of God's blessings. Perhaps the greatest reward that comes to one who sincerely occupies himself with worthy causes is the beneficial effect it has upon his children who are thereby inspired to do likewise.

God said to Abraham, *"Take, I pray thee (Na) your son . . . and get thee (Lech Le'cha) into the land of Moriah, and offer him there as a burnt offering."*

> The word *Na* denotes pleading. God pleaded with Abraham, "I have tested you with several tests and you have withstood them all. Now, I beg you to withstand this test also, for otherwise it will be said that the previous tests were of no value (Sanhedrin 89b).

No matter how much a person has accomplished, he cannot rest upon his laurels. He must prove himself loyal and steadfast in each and every situation lest, by faltering even once in faith and devotion, he undo all that he has accomplished. In fact, the more one has achieved, the greater the disappointment and the more damaging the impact upon others if he fails to live up to expectations even once.

What is the meaning of the word *Moriah?* One Sage explains it as the place from which instruction (*Ho'ra'ah*) goes forth to the world. (It was there that the Temple stood in later times and from there the Great Sanhedrin sent forth religious teaching). Another Sage explained Moriah as the place from which religious awe (*Yirah*) goes forth to the world (Genesis Rabbah).

The site where Abraham proved himself ready to sacrifice his most priceless possession ultimately became the site of the Holy Temple; indicating that it is only when a person is ready to give his all for his faith, that his worship and offerings to the Lord have meaning.

Notice, also, that from the site of the Temple, religious teachings and awe go forth to the world. The religious teachings, the sense of awe and reverence that permeate the Temple, must radiate outward and have a profound impact upon the entire world. The significance of a House of Worship is not to be found in what goes on inside but in the effect that it has upon the world outside, in the effect that it has upon the worshipper after he leaves the Temple and goes about his daily tasks.

The *land of Moriah* is Jerusalem as we are told specifically in Second Chronicles, "Then Solomon began to build the house of the Lord at Jerusalem in Mount Moriah" (3:1)—(Rashi).

God's command to Abraham concerning his son, Isaac, is thus the first contact of the Jewish people with the holy city of Jerusalem and it was a contact that required willingness to make the greatest sacrifice. Throughout history, the Jew has been called upon to sacrifice to possess Jerusalem and has been willing to do so. In 1948, superhuman effort was expended to keep the road to Jerusalem open and thus save at least New Jerusalem from falling into the hands of the Arabs. During the Six Day War of June 1967, hundreds of the finest young men of Israel gave their lives so that all of Jerusalem could once again be united under Jewish rule. Undoubtedly, there would have been far fewer casualties had Israel been willing to use the planes and artillery that were so effective elsewhere; but to spare Jerusalem from destruction, Israel refrained from doing so even though it meant the sacrifice of many Jewish lives.

This is the second occasion that the Torah uses the phrase *Lech Le'cha*, "Get thee." The first was when God appeared to Abraham for the first time and told him, *"Get thee out of thy land."* Of the two two occasions we do not know which is more precious in the eyes of God, the first or the second. However, from the wording here, *"Get thee into the land of Moriah"* it follows that the second occasion was more precious than the first (Genesis Rabbah).

There are many people who hear the call, *"Get thee out";* they know that they are dissatisfied with things as they are. Unfortunately, however they do not hear the call, *"Get thee into the land of Moriah."* They have no Moriah, no goal, no ideal that they are striving to attain. They know only what they do *not* want; they have no vision of what they *do* want. That is why so much of the Protest Movement in our country and throughout the world is negative and destructive in character, rather than positive and constructive. It is far easier to agree that a structure should be torn down than to agree on what type of new structure should replace it. However, if true progress is to be achieved, we must progress from the concept of *Get thee out* to the concept of *Get thee into*. It may be more difficult but it is also more important, and therefore "more precious in the eyes of God," that we strive to attain Moriah, that we adopt positive and constructive goals and ideals for the future.

Abraham Meets the Test

22:3-5

And Abraham rose early in the morning and saddled his ass.

Why *early in the morning?* Because the eagerly devout perform the *mitzvot* at the earliest possible moment (Tanchuma).

A person who loves God's commandments and accepts God's will does not delay what is required of him even when it is most painful. How much less justification for delay, then, when fulfilling the *mitzvot* requires little or no sacrifice on our part!

Abraham saddled his own donkey. Why? Surely he had plenty of slaves? But his love of God upset the natural order. The Gentile prophet Balaam also saddled his own donkey when he set out to curse the Israelites at the behest of Balak, King of Moab (Numbers 22:21). He too had plenty of slaves but it was his hatred of Israel that upset the natural order. Thus we see that both love and hate can upset the natural order (Genesis Rabbah).

Both love and hate can lead people to do that which ordinarily they would never think of doing. They are opposite sides of the same coin and have a powerful and sometimes irrational impact upon the way we act. A person propelled by love is willing to do almost anything for the object of his love, but, unfortunately, the converse is also true. How much more praiseworthy it is when our extraordinary efforts are motivated by love rather than hate!

Abraham's donkey was the very same donkey that Moses rode when he returned to Egypt to undertake the redemption of his people and it is upon this same donkey that the Messiah, son of David, will ride in the future. This extraordinary donkey was created at twilight on the sixth day of Creation (Pirkei d'Rabbi Eliezer).

Abraham on his way to sacrifice Isaac, and Moses on his way to Egypt to emancipate his people both rode upon the same donkey. In this fanciful flight of imagination our Sages are telling us that both Abraham and Moses were impelled and driven by the same force; a willingness to sacrifice all in the service of God. The Messiah will also ride upon that self-same donkey, for the redemption of the future can only be achieved by a complete spirit of self-sacrifice in the service of the Almighty. This spirit of self-sacrifice that exists in a few truly dedicated individuals harks back to the time of Creation, being created almost simultaneously with Man, for without such dedication mankind could have achieved little that was significant and worthwhile.

On the third day Abraham looked up and saw the place from afar. Then Abraham said to his servants, "You stay here with the ass. The boy and I will go up there."

> Why on the third day and not on the first or second day? It was in order that the people of the world might not say that Abraham slaughtered his son in a moment of confusion (Tanchuma).

The Binding of Isaac was not an impetuous, hasty decision made on the spur of the moment which Abraham would have rejected had he had time for more mature consideration. Even after three days and in full possession of his faculties, Abraham was prepared to do the bidding of his God.

It is relatively easy to be caught up in the enthusiasm of the moment or to respond nobly at a time of crisis. It is much more difficult to maintain a sense of dedication and spirit of sacrifice after the momentary crisis or enthusiasm has passed. For example, the devotion and sacrifice of American Jews during the crisis of the Six Day War was most commendable but the real test of our devotion to Israel is whether we can maintain that spirit of devotion and sacrifice over a long period of time. True devotion to an ideal is manifested by unwavering determination that withstands the challenge of time and is not subject to short peaks of enthusiasm followed by lengthy periods of apathy and indifference.

The journey took three days because of the various obstacles that had to be overcome. For example, after failing to dissuade Abraham from starting out on his journey, Satan transformed himself into a great river which had to be crossed to reach Moriah. The waters reached up to their necks before Abraham and Isaac succeeded in traversing it (Tanchuma).

Satan also appeared to Abraham disguised as an old man and said to him, "Would an old man like yourself destroy this precious son whom the Almighty has given you in your old age?" (Midrash Va'yosha).

There are various obstacles that can deter an individual from fulfilling what he knows to be God's commandment. These obstacles can be in the form of a "river"—external hindrances that appear to be insurmountable and therefore cause the faint-hearted to turn back from their declared intention. They can also be in the form of an "old man"—internal barriers such as the feeling, "I am too old" or "there is no time." Abraham overcame both types of obstacle. We, too, must not allow ourselves to be deterred from doing that which we know we should do, by the obstacles, either internal or external, that lie in our path.

And saw the place from afar. What did he see? He saw a cloud enveloping the mountain and recognizing it as the cloud of God's glory he exclaimed, "That must be the place where God told me to sacrifice my son." Turning to Isaac, he asked, "My son, do you see what I see?" "Yes," replied Isaac. Then turning to his two servants, he asked them the same question, "Do you see what I see?" and they answered, "No, we see nothing." Exclaimed Abraham, "You do not see just as the donkey does not see; therefore, *'You stay here with the ass. The boy and I will go up there'* " (Genesis Rabbah).

There was nothing wrong with the eyesight of Abraham's two servants. Abraham rebuked them because they failed to see "the cloud of God's glory"; they could not see the manifestation of the divine in all that was happening. Only Isaac could perceive "God's glory" in what was happening.

Our generation has been privileged to witness a truly miraculous event, the establishment of the State of Israel after 2,000 years of exile and homelessness. Unfortunately, the nations of the world, like Abraham's two servants, have been unable to see "the cloud of God's glory" hovering over the events of our day; they fail to see in the establishment of Israel and the Unification of Jerusalem manifestations of the Divine Presence. Even many Jews have remained blind to the nature of the events unfolding before their very eyes.

Who were the two servants? Ishmael and Eliezer (Genesis Rabbah).

Ishmael was one of the servants who had accompanied Abraham and Isaac. All looked at the same thing; yet Ishmael saw only an ordinary mountain while Abraham and Isaac saw something beautiful and inspiring.

In the decades preceding the establishment of the Jewish state, the Arabs, who are the descendants of Ishmael, saw in Palestine only barren deserts and desolate, rock-strewn hills and mountains. They did not believe that the country could be made to bloom. The result was *You stay here with the ass.* They made little or no progress and the land remained barren and desolate. The descendants of Isaac, however, came to the land with a noble vision. They, too, saw the desolate mountains and deserts but they were able to look beyond these to see "a beautiful mountain with the cloud of God's glory enveloping it." They had the vision to see the fertile fields and the blooming gardens that could be made out of the barren wilderness and, impelled by this vision, they succeeded in making the desert bloom.

Progress can be brought about only by those with the vision to look beyond the mountains of obstacles and hardships to perceive what can be achieved through sacrifice, hard work and devotion.

"We will worship and we will return to you."

It was only through the merit of worship that Abraham and Isaac were able to return unharmed from the ordeal on Mount Moriah (Genesis Rabbah).

Since the time of the *Akedah* the Jewish people has undergone innumerable trials and ordeals, persecutions, pogroms and holocausts. Like Isaac they have managed to survive and to emerge spiritually unscathed, primarily due to the strength, comfort and courage they received from prayer and worship.

The Role of Isaac

22:6-10

Abraham took the wood for the burnt offering and put it on his son Isaac.

Abraham did not hesitate to place the burden of responsibility on young shoulders. He did not seek to spare his son the hard work and the discipline that forge one's character and shape one's personality.

Parents today, and especially Jewish parents, are noted for the sacrifices that they make for their children in order that their children may have everything. What is required today, however, is not just sacrifice *for* children but sacrifice *of* children; not physical sacrifice of course like that of the *Akedah* but the making of demands upon them, the placing of burdens upon them, making them face up while yet young to the obligations and responsibilities of life. When enlisted in an exciting cause, in a worthwhile struggle, the youth of today, like Isaac, are capable of all of the idealism and all of the sacrifice that are required.

He himself took the firestone and the knife and the two walked off together.

Hand in hand, as one person (Midrash HaGadol).

There was an admirable spirit of unity between father and son, between the older and the younger generation. One of the most vexing problems of society today is the ever widening "generation gap" between parents and children. Abraham, having trained Isaac from the very beginning in the performance of *mitzvot*, succeeded with him where he had failed with his oldest son, Ishmael.

One of the reasons Isaac turned out as well as he did was that his father not only "sent him" to perform *mitzvot* but "walked with him." It has been well observed, "Train a child in the way he should go, and walk there yourself once in a while." Undoubtedly, the Generation Gap today would not be as wide as it is, if young people did not sense such a gap between the professed values of their parents and their actions.

Perhaps the reason the phrase *And the two walked together* is repeated (here and verse 8) is that it expresses both the ideal we hope to achieve and at the same time the best way to bring about the realization of that ideal.

Then Isaac said to his father, ". . . Here is the firestone and the wood; but where is the sheep for the burnt offering?"

> When Isaac asked this question, Abraham replied, "My son, you are the burnt offering." At that moment Abraham was troubled, thinking that perhaps Isaac would run away. Said Isaac to him, "Father, do not fear. May it be God's will that my blood be acceptable unto Him. However, bind me well so that I do not move. Also, when you return to my mother, Sarah, do not break the news to her abruptly lest she injure herself. If she is standing on the roof or next to a pit, she may fall or jump and be killed. If she has a knife in her hand she may kill herself with it." Isaac went along with Abraham with his mouth but in his heart he was saying, "Who will save me from my father? I have no other help but God, as it is said, 'My help cometh from the Lord who made heaven and earth'" (Psalm 121:2)— (Avot d'Rabbi Nathan).

Even when his life was in mortal danger, Isaac's main concern was not for his own safety but for his parents. He did not want his father to be troubled on his account and at the same time he was concerned about the effect that his death would have upon his aged mother, Sarah. Isaac's concern for his parents is most touching and his desire to cushion the terrible shock to his mother is most admirable.

Isaac's behavior throughout the terrible ordeal is truly remarkable and the fact that in his heart he hoped to be saved does not make his actions any less praiseworthy. Isaac was willing to do whatever his father asked of him but, while the breath of life was still in him, it was only natural and right that he should hope and pray that his life be spared. Isaac looked for his salvation to the Almighty, recognizing that "My help cometh from the Lord." Although we should be ready to accept martyrdom and death when necessary, we must never abandon the will to live.

And Abraham said, "God will see to the sheep for His burnt offering, my son."

> *God will see*—in the future—at the time of the Exodus from Egypt. *For when the Lord goes through to smite the Egyptians, He will see the blood on the lintel and the two doorposts, and the Lord will pass over the door and not let the Destroyer enter and smite your home* (Exodus 12:23). What blood will He see at that time? The blood of the sacrifice of Isaac. In addition, concerning the destruction that God intended to bring in the time of King David, the Bible says, *And as He was about to destroy, the Lord beheld and He repented Him"* (I Chronicles 21:5). What did He behold? He beheld the blood of the sacrifice of Isaac, as it says, *"God will see to the sheep for His burnt offering, my son"* (Mechilta, Bo, 11).

The merit of the *Akedah* as a reason for God to show compassion to the People of Israel is a recurrent theme in the High Holy Day liturgy. Though we have sinned and are lacking in merit we have the right to hope for the mercy of God because of the merit of our righteous ancestors; Abraham, who was willing to sacrifice his son at God's command, and Isaac, who stood ready to be sacrificed.

When the Temple was destroyed, Abraham began to plead before God, "King of the Universe, when I was 100 years old You gave me a son. When he already had a mind of his own, being a young man of 37, You commanded me, 'Offer him as a sacrifice.' I steeled my heart against him and had no compassion on him, but myself bound him to the altar. Will you not remember this on my behalf and have mercy on my children?" Isaac, also, began to speak before God, "King of the Universe, when my father said to me, *'God will see to the sheep for His burnt offering, my son'* and I realized that I was to be the offering, I raised no objection to the carrying out of Your words. I willingly let myself be bound on the top of the altar and stretched out my neck beneath the knife. Will You not remember this on my behalf and have mercy on my children?" (Echah Rabba, Prologue 24).

Not only do we constantly refer to the *Akedah* in pleading for God's compassion on the High Holy Days, but Abraham and Isaac, as well, plead on our behalf using the argument of the merit of the *Akedah*. Our righteous ancestors plead our cause before the throne of the Almighty and, therefore, we have reason to hope that our sins shall indeed be forgiven.

According to the Midrash, Isaac was not a young child at the time of the *Akedah* but a grown man of 37 with a mind of his own; yet he willingly accepted the authority of his father. The commandment, "Honor thy father and thy mother" is not meant for youngsters only; even adults, with families of their own, owe respect and obedience to parents.

They arrived at the place of which God had told him and Abraham built the altar there.

Notice that the text does not say that Abraham

170

built "an altar" but that he built *"the altar"* (*Ha'-miz'be'ach*). The definite article is used because it was the same altar upon which Adam had sacrificed, as well as Cain and Abel and Noah and his sons (Pirkei d'Rabbi Eliezer).

The building of an altar and the offering of a sacrifice to God was not something that was original with Abraham; from the very beginning of history men offered sacrifices to their gods. It was the *nature* of Abraham's sacrifice that was different. Before the time of Noah, people offered sacrifices simply as a means of bargaining with God or the gods. It was strictly a quid pro quo arrangement in which the individual clearly expected something in return. Noah was the first to offer a sacrifice as an expression of gratitude to God for having spared him and his family. Abraham, however, was the first to offer a sacrifice which was neither a request for God's favor or even an expression of gratitude for a favor already received but simply a manifestation of love for God and of unquestioning obedience to His will without any thought of favor or reward. Our prayers and material offerings to God fall most frequently into the category of asking for a favor, less frequently into the category of gratefulness for blessings received and all too rarely are they the type of offering made by Abraham; an expression of our love for God without any thought of reward expected or received.

He bound his son Isaac.

When Abraham wanted to sacrifice Isaac, the latter said to him, "Father, I am a young man and I am afraid that my body may tremble through fear of the knife and I will cause you grief. The slaughter may thereby be rendered unfit and not count as a real sacrifice. Therefore, bind me very firmly." Forthwith, *He bound Isaac.* Can one bind a man 37 years old without his consent? (Genesis Rabbah).

Throughout the entire *Akedah*, Isaac participated knowingly and willingly. Although his role was largely a passive

171

one, he is as much the hero of the *Akedah* as is his father, Abraham. Had not Isaac been willing to obey his father and fulfill God's commands, Abraham, with all his love of God, could never have fulfilled the command of God.

We are in the habit of castigating young people today for failure to heed their parents but we should not lose sight of the many fine young people who follow willingly their parents' noblest traditions. Young people cannot be compelled or coerced into doing the wishes of their parents. They must be motivated from the very beginning to *want* to do so.

> We are commanded, *"You must love the Lord your God with all your heart and with all your soul and with all your might"* (Deuteronomy 6:5). *With all your soul* means like Isaac who bound himself upon the altar (Sifrei, Devarim 32).

Isaac was only the first of countless Jews throughout the ages who were willing to give up their lives *Al Kiddush Hashem,* for the sanctification of God's Name. We are told that when Rabbi Akiba was brought out to be executed by the Romans and saw his disciples weeping bitterly, he comforted them and bade them not to weep for him. "All my life," he told them, "I fulfilled the command to love God *with all my heart* and *with all my might.* Now that I have the opportunity to demonstrate that I also love God *with all my soul,* I am able to die content."

And Abraham picked up the knife to slay his son.

> The angels of heaven cried out to God, "Behold, the knife is upon his neck! How long are You going to wait?" (Pesikta Rabati 40).

Unfortunately, this anguished cry has been heard time and time again throughout our history. It has welled up from the stake of the auto-da-fè and the rack of the Inquisition, from the rubble of the pogrom and from the gas chambers and crematoria of the Holocaust. "How long, O Lord, how long!"

172

God Intercedes

22:11-12

Then an angel of the Lord called to him from Heaven: "Abraham, Abraham."

> The repetition of the name here, as well as in the case of Jacob, Moses and Samuel, indicates that they remained the same after God had spoken to them as they had been before (Sifra, Vayikra I).

The greatest of men are generally the humblest of men, not blown up with their own importance. The truly great man is the same after success as before, remaining modest and humble as did the great Patriarchs of our people.

> The repetition also indicates that God spoke not only to Abraham but to future generations as well. There is no generation that does not contain men like Abraham and there is no generation that does not contain men like Jacob, Moses and Samuel (Genesis Rabbah)

We tend to glorify the past at the expense of the present, extolling the wisdom and virtues of the great men of the past while intimating that such men are no longer to be found. The truth is that each generation produces righteous, God fearing men and women to whom "God speaks" and who are ever ready to answer the Divine call with *Hi'ne'ni*, "Here I am."

And he answered, "Here I am" (Hi'ne'ni).

> Moses answered *Hi'ne'ni* when God called to him from the burning bush (Exodus 3:4). Said God to him, "You are following in the footsteps of Abraham who was the first to answer in this manner" (Exodus Rabbah 2).

The greatness of an Abraham or a Moses lay precisely in the fact that they heard the voice of God summoning them

173

to their responsibility and they answered *Hi'ne'ni*. When we hear the voice of duty calling to us, we, too, must be able to answer *"Here I am"* and not shirk the call by false appeals to humility or inadequacy.

And the angel said, *"Do not raise your hand against the boy or do anything to him."*

> Said God to Abraham, "When I commanded you, *"Take your son"* I did not tell you to slaughter him but only to *take him up* upon the altar. You have fulfilled My command. Now take him down" (Genesis Rabbah).

God, of course, abhors human sacrifice and the story of the *Akedah* is meant as a ringing, definitive protest against this monstrous practice that was so widespread in the ancient world. It took centuries to uproot completely the pagan practice of human sacrifice. An indication of the abhorrence with which Jews looked upon such sacrifice can be found in the Hebrew word for "hell" which is *Gehinnom*. The word derives from *Gai Ben-Hinnom*, the Valley of Ben Hinnom, outside of Jerusalem where children were sacrificed to the idol Moloch (cf. II Kings 23:10). Although the story of the *Akedah* teaches many positive values, its first and foremost message is an unequivocal condemnation of human sacrifice.

We moderns smugly feel that the sacrifice of our young to Moloch is one sin of which we are most certainly not guilty. What else but that, however, can one call the sending off of our young to be slaughtered in senseless wars fought not for survival but for "glory" or in the name of "national honor."

"For now I know that you fear God, since you have not withheld your son, your favored one, from Me."

> Said Abraham to God, "Master of the Universe, a man will test another in order to ascertain what is in his heart but You, who know the innermost thoughts of man, did You have to test me in this

manner? Did You not know how I would react?" God replied, "Of course I knew but my purpose was to let the people of the world know that I had not chosen you without cause (Tanchuma).

God does not test man in order that He may know, for God is All-Knowing, but in order that man may know. Without the *Akedah*, we would not have this inspiring example of Abraham's complete submission to God and willingness to obey God's command. The *Akedah* has served as a constant source of inspiration throughout the ages. God's test of Abraham served not to increase God's knowledge of man but man's knowledge of God and what He requires of us.

> The fear of God spoken of here refers to reverence of God out of love and not out of fear for it is written, "the seed of Abraham who loves Me" (Isaiah 41:8). Greater is the one who serves God out of love than the one who serves God out of fear (Sotah 31a).

Abraham's religion was based upon love of God rather than upon fear of God. The true believer serves God not out of fear that he will be punished if he fails to do so, and not even out of hope of reward but out of pure, disinterested love, without any ulterior motive. Pirkei Avot bids us, "Be not like slaves who minister to the master for the sake of receiving a reward, but be like slaves who minister to the master not for the sake of receiving a reward" (1:3). Too often, today, our religion, like that of the ancient heathen, is based upon fear. We should strive to attain the level of an Abraham who served God out of love. Twice each day the pious Jew recites the words of the *Shema*, "You must love the Lord your God" (Deut. 6:5).

The Ram's Horn

22:13

And Abraham lifted up his eyes and looked and behold behind him a ram (Ayil Achar) caught in the thicket by his horns.

This ram had been created on the sixth day of Creation, on the eve of the Sabbath at twilight (Avot 5:9).

From the very beginning, God had provided the ram which ultimately would be sacrificed in place of Isaac. In other words, long before Abraham was subjected to the test, God had prepared his deliverance. At a time of deep distress we may not be able to imagine how we can possibly be saved but it is possible that, unbeknown to us, God has already provided the means of our deliverance.

All that day Abraham saw the ram become entangled in a tree, extricate itself, then become entangled in a bush and extricate itself again. This happened again and again. Said God to Abraham, "Abraham, so will it be with your descendants. They will be entangled in their sins and, therefore, will fall into the clutches of one tyrannical power after another; Babylonia, Media, Greece and Rome." Whereupon Abraham exclaimed, "Master of the Universe, shall it ever be thus?" and God answered, "In the end they will be redeemed through the horns of this ram" (Genesis Rabbah).

Throughout history, great and powerful empires have sought to destroy the Jewish people but the Jew has survived all persecution and attempts at genocide and has lived to be redeemed in our day. What enabled the Jewish people to survive when mightier nations have disappeared? Undoubtedly, they survived "through the horns of this ram" which symbolizes willingness to sacrifice everything for one's faith. It was the Jew's willingness to make the su-

176

preme sacrifice, if need be, that enabled him to survive and to be redeemed.

What does *Achar* mean? After all (*Achar*) that God has done for Israel, they still fall into the clutches of sin and in consequence become victims of persecution; yet they will ultimately be saved by the ram's horn. Throughout the year Jews are in the clutches of sin and led astray by their troubles, but on Rosh Hashanah they take the Shofar and blow on it, and eventually they will be redeemed by the ram's horn (Genesis Rabbah).

The sounds of the Shofar on Rosh Hashanah summon us to extricate ourselves from sin and to lead better lives. In the words of Maimonides, the Shofar calls to us, "Awake ye sleepers from your slumber and rouse you from your lethargy. Scrutinize your deeds and return in repentance. Look well into your souls and mend your ways and your actions. Let each one of you forsake his evil path and his unworthy purpose and return to God." If we truly heeded the sound of the Shofar we would indeed be redeemed from sin.

God said to Abraham, "Your children are destined to sin in the future and I will sit in judgment upon them on Rosh Hashanah. However, if they want Me to forgive them, they should blow the Shofar before Me on that day." Said Abraham, "What is a Shofar?" "You mean you do not know?" "No," replied Abraham. Whereupon God said, "Turn behind you and look." *And Abraham lifted up his eyes and looked and behold behind him a ram caught in the thicket by his horns.* Said God to him, "Let them blow before Me with this horn and I will forgive their sins" (Tanchuma).

Why do Jews blow a Shofar made out of a ram's horn on Rosh Hashanah? It is in order that God may remember for them the *Akedah* of Isaac and account it to them as if they had sacrificed themselves before Him (Rosh Hashanah 16a).

The blowing of the Shofar on Rosh Hashanah recalls the *Akedah* and the ram offered up by Abraham in place of his son. It calls upon us to remember this event and to be inspired by the wholehearted devotion to God of our ancestors, Abraham and Isaac, thus ensuring that our sins be forgiven. It also calls upon God to remember the merit of our righteous ancestors and to have mercy upon us for their sake, if not for ours.

> What does *Achar* (after) refer to? After God saw that Abraham was ready to sacrifice his son Isaac "with all his heart and soul," he sent the ram as a substitute for Isaac (Tanchuma, Tsav 13).

It is the readiness to sacrifice all that is ours for what we believe that frequently renders such supreme sacrifice unnecessary, for only when we are prepared to sacrifice greatly does deliverance come.

> Nothing of that ram went to waste. Its ashes later became the foundation of the inner altar upon which atonement was made for Israel on the Day of Atonement. Out of its sinews were made the ten strings of David's harp and the skin was used for the girdle worn by Elijah. As for its two horns, the left one was sounded at the giving of the Torah on Mt. Sinai and the right one, which is even larger than the left, will be sounded in that future time of the Ingathering of Exiles (Pirkei d'Rabbi Eliezer).

The strings of David's harp recall the voice of the Jew raised in song and prayer to his God. Elijah, of course, was the prophet who in his uncompromising devotion to social justice dared to confront even the King with the accusation, "Have you murdered and also taken possession?" (I Kings 21:19). The horns of the ram symbolize, say our Sages, the giving of the Torah and the return to Zion. It is these four factors—acceptance of the Torah, prayer to the Almighty, devotion to the ideals of social justice and the yearning to return to Zion—that were, in the words of the Midrash, "the foundation of the inner altar upon which atonement was made for Israel." These are the things that enabled the Jewish people to surmount all adversity and to survive in the past and these are the elements that remain essential to Jewish survival to this day.

The Lord Will See

22:14

And Abraham named that site Adonai-Yireh (the Lord will see).

Said Abraham, "O God, when You asked for the sacrifice of Isaac, I might have retorted, 'Lord of the Universe, a little while ago you assured me, *It is through Isaac that offspring shall be continued for you* (21:12) ; now You say, *Take your son . . . and offer him.*' But I restrained myself and said nothing. Even so, may it be Thy will, O Lord our God, that when Isaac's children are in trouble You will remember that binding in their favor and have mercy on them" (Genesis Rabbah).

Abraham prayed that the Lord would see and be mindful of his unquestioning obedience and that the merit of his unwavering faith would win forgiveness for his descendants. This is a major theme of our High Holy Day liturgy as we pray that our sounding of the Shofar will cause God to be mindful of the merit of our ancestors and thus have mercy upon us.

We see here that Abraham called the place which was later the site of the Temple *Yireh* while Shem had originally called it *Salem.* This posed a dilemma for God. Said He, "If I call it *Salem,* as did Shem, I am annulling the words of Abraham My Friend who called it *Yireh,* while if I use the name *Yireh* I am annulling the words of the righteous Shem who called it *Salem.*" What then did God do? He combined the names given to the place by Abraham and

179

Shem and called it Jerusalem. What is Jerusalem? *Yireh Salem,* "will see peace" (Midrash T'hillim 76).

Jerusalem is the Holy City but throughout most of its history it has not been permitted to be a City of Peace. Assyrians, Babylonians, Romans, Moslems, Crusaders, Turks and modern day Arabs have all either laid her waste or laid seige to her. Now that Jerusalem is reunited in the hands of those who love her, and barbed wire and military fortifications no longer divide and disfigure the city, it should be the profound hope and prayer of all men of good will that Jerusalem at last *Yireh Salem* "will see peace"; that not only may "Peace be within thy walls and prosperity within thy palaces" (Ps. 122:7) but that from Jerusalem true and lasting peace may go forth to all of mankind.

As it is said to this day: "On the mount of the Lord there is vision."

> What is the significance of the words *this day?* It means, "as on this day" for the day on which the *Akedah* took place was Rosh Hashanah (Pesikta Rabati).

Not only do we read the story of the *Akedah* on Rosh Hashanah but according to tradition the event occurred on Rosh Hashanah. Thus the story is read in the synagogue on the very anniversary of the event.

> Literally, the text reads "as it is said this day" thus teaching that Abraham already knew that this would be the site of the House of Worship in future generations (Midrash HaGadol).

From the moment that Abraham showed such great faith and devotion at that spot, it was fore-ordained that the Temple would be built there. A House of God can be erected only where there is devotion and a willingness to sacrifice.

> Not only did Abraham see in his mind's eye the Temple but he also saw it destroyed and rebuilt (Genesis Rabbah).

The history of a House of Worship is very rarely a straight line of uninterrupted progress and growth. There are bound to be setbacks and defeats. The true believer, however, can take in stride the setbacks without becoming discouraged and can see in his mind's eye the realization of the goal toward which he is dedicating his efforts.

God's Promise

22:15-19

The angel of the Lord called to Abraham a second time from heaven, and said, "By Myself I swear, the Lord declares...."

What is the need for this oath? Abraham had pleaded with God, "Swear to me that You will not test me or my son Isaac anymore." He had undergone ten trials and now wanted God to promise not to test him yet again. The *Akedah* was the tenth trial and it was equal to all of the others put together (Genesis Rabbah).

The Jewish people has undergone numerous tests of its loyalty to God through the ages. Equal to all of the others put together in severity was the trial of the Holocaust in which six million Jews lost their lives. Through all these trials the Jewish people emerged unshaken in faith, but now we have the right to plead with God as did Abraham, "Swear to us that You will not test us or our children anymore." We have earned the right to live in peace, developing our own distinctive way of life, without undergoing further trials and tribulations in which we must prove our faith in God in the midst of crushing adversity.

"Because you have done this and have not withheld your son, your favored one, I will bestow My blessing upon you."

Since Abraham had undergone ten trials, why does God say to him, *"Because you have done this ... I will bestow My blessing upon you"?* It was because had Abraham not withstood this test, he would have lost everything (Genesis Rabbah).

Although Abraham had surmounted successfully nine different ordeals, all would have been for naught had he not withstood the tenth. There are those who after having overcome numerous difficulties allow themselves to become discouraged and give up, unaware that the goal they seek is just around the corner. Had Abraham not possessed the quality of perseverance, he would have lost the reward for all that he had previously achieved. God's blessing is bestowed upon the individual who is able to persevere through all difficulties and obstacles. Suddenly he finds that the hardships are now behind him and he may enjoy God's blessing in peace.

"And make your descendants as numerous as the stars of heaven and the sands on the seashore."

Israel is compared to the stars of heaven because they are destined to shine as brightly as stars (Midrash HaGadol).

The prophet refers to Israel as "a light of the nations" (Isaiah 49:6). It is the prophetic mission of the Jew to bring the light of human dignity and ethical living, as found in our tradition, to the entire world.

Why is Israel compared to both *the stars of heaven* and *the sands on the seashore?* Because when Israel does the will of God, they are like *the stars of heaven,* not under the domination of any nation or people; but when they transgress God's will, then they are like *the sands on the seashore* which can easily be trampled underfoot (Or Ha'afelah).

The fate of the Jewish people is determined by its relationship to God. Faith in God and adherence to His commandments are the most powerful defensive weapons that we Jews possess. When we shed these moral armaments then we are easy prey for any who would seek to trample upon us.

Israel is compared here to *the sands on the sea-shore.* Just as the sand serves as a barrier to the raging sea and the waves break as they reach the sand, so is it with Israel. The nations of the world raise themselves up against Israel but in the end are "broken" before him. So it was with Pharaoh, Sisera, Babylon, Haman and the Greeks and so will it be with Rome (Midrash Aggadah).

The quiet sands of the sea may appear to be no match for the billowing waves of a raging sea but the waves break upon the sand and cannot permanently destroy it. Throughout history, tyrants have attempted to destroy the Jewish people but not only have they ultimately failed, they have "broken" themselves in the process.

"All the nations of the earth shall bless themselves by your descendants."

Just as without the soil of the earth the world could not exist, for without soil there can be no trees and no produce, so without Israel the world could not exist, as it says, *"All the nations of the earth shall bless themselves by your descendants"* (Pesikta Rabati 11).

The soil of the earth is taken for granted, trod upon and looked down upon, yet it is essential for human existence. The Jewish people have been scorned, despised and trampled upon, yet without the Jew the world could not exist, for it is the Jewish people that have given to the world the principles of ethics and morality that it needs to survive.

Abraham then returned to his servants.

Where then was Isaac? Abraham had sent him to the Academy of Shem to study Torah. Said Abraham, "All that has come to me has come only because I have busied myself with Torah and good deeds. Therefore, I do not want these to ever depart from my descendants" (Genesis Rabbah).

We Jews are a people only by virtue of the Torah. It is the Torah that sets us apart from all other peoples and that is responsible for all that we are and for our very existence as a people. It is, therefore, incumbent upon us to make every sacrifice in order to insure that the Torah will never be forgotten by our children. Jewish education must be given the highest priority in our scale of values and we must strive to insure that every Jewish youngster receive as intensive a Jewish education as possible.

The Birth of Rebecca

22:20-24

The story of the *Akedah* is followed immediately by Abraham's being informed of the descendants of his brother Nachor; including the birth of Rebecca, his brother's granddaughter.

> After the *Akedah*, Abraham began to worry about the future of his son. Who would Isaac marry? One of the Canaanite women? Therefore, while yet on Mount Moriah, he was informed that Isaac's mate had been born (Lekach Tov).

Abraham, the first Jewish parent, was greatly worried lest his child marry a Canaanite woman. Jewish parents today are beset with the same worry. Parents who are concerned about little else Jewishly, are alarmed at the prospect of their children marrying out of the faith. Unlike Abraham, however, they do little or nothing to reduce the likelihood of intermarriage.

> We are told here of the birth of Rebecca before we read of the death of Sarah in the next chapter because before God causes the sun of one righteous individual to set, He causes the sun of another righteous individual to rise. Before Sarah died, Rebecca was born, and so throughout Jewish history; before

the sun of one great leader set, the sun of his successor had risen (Genesis Rabbah).

God never leaves His people without leaders and men of learning. No man or woman is irreplaceable. The great men and women of one generation are followed by the great men and women of the next generation. Life goes on! Death is a grievous blow but there is always somebody capable of taking the place of the deceased, as head of the family or of the entire people.

CHAPTER 13

The Death of Sarah

23:1-2

Sarah's lifetime—the span of Sarah's life—came to one hundred and twenty-seven years.

Literally, the Hebrew text reads that the life of Sarah was "a hundred years and twenty years and seven years." Why this seemingly superfluous repetition of the word "years" after each number? It is to indicate that at the age of 20 she was as at the age of 7 in beauty; and at the age of 100 she was as at the age of 20 in regard to sin (Genesis Rabbah).

Since it is hardly surprising that a girl of 20 should be beautiful and a woman of 100 without sin, a variant reading that "at the age of 100 she was as at 20 in beauty and at the age of 20 she was as at the age of 7 in regard to sin" (Lekach Tov), has usually seemed preferable. The text would then indicate that as a young woman Sarah was as chaste and innocent as a child and that as an old woman she still retained the beauty of her youth.

The original text, however, also contains a valid lesson. The statement that "at the age of 20 she was as at the age of 7 in regard to beauty" can refer to the fact that just as the beauty of a 7-year-old is a natural beauty, not dependent upon make-up and artificial beauty aids, so Sarah at the age of 20 was satisfied with natural beauty and did not have recourse to all sorts of make-up and cosmetics to make her what she was not. Unfortunately, many young women today, in their desire to appear glamorous, overdo the use of cosmetics to the point where they cheapen rather than enhance their natural attractiveness.

The assertion that "at the age of 100 Sarah was as at the age of 20 in regard to sin" indicates that throughout life she remained pure and innocent and has reference to the tradition that until the age of 20 an individual is not held liable for his or her sins (Rashi). Although youthful offenders today are supposed to receive special treatment in our courts, it is unfortunately true that a youthful indiscretion can destroy a person for life. Our Sages obviously felt that the youth of an offender should be taken into consideration and that no one should have to suffer throughout life for an offense committed as a result of youth and immaturity.

Why is the word "years" repeated in the text? To indicate that at the age of 7 Sarah had the knowledge of a 20 year old while at the age of 20 she possessed the righteousness usually associated with an old woman of 100 (Midrash HaGadol).

Sarah was not only precocious as a child but her moral character also developed at an early age. There is nothing remarkable about an older person living righteously but one does not ordinarily associate righteousness with youth. A young person who possesses the wisdom and maturity to live righteously and whose moral character is well developed, indeed is much to be praised.

And Abraham came to mourn for Sarah and to weep for her.

From where did he come? He came from Mt. Moriah where he had gone to sacrifice Isaac. Sarah, thinking that Isaac had been sacrificed, died of grief. This is why the account of the death of Sarah is placed immediately after the account of the *Akedah* (Genesis Rabbah).

It was the wicked angel Samael who made it his business to tell Sarah that Abraham had cruelly offered up a protesting Isaac as a sacrifice; whereupon, she died of shock and grief. When Abraham returned from Mt. Moriah with Isaac, he found her already dead (Pirkei d'Rabbi Eliezer).

There are always people who delight in being the first to relay bad news or to bring the latest malicious gossip. The Samaels of our time cause untold grief and anguish by gleefully reporting unsubstantiated rumors or distressing news to unwary people; all in the name of "telling the truth" or being "frank even if it hurts."

From the fact that Sarah's funeral was delayed until Abraham could return from Mt. Moriah we can learn that the eulogy and the funeral service is for the sake of the living rather than for the sake of the dead (Sanhedrin 46b).

The purpose of all the Jewish rituals of mourning is to enable the bereaved to confront their grief and to surmount it. An effective eulogy is not one that tears at the heartstrings of the mourners but one that brings them some measure of comfort and consolation. One who officiates at funerals must always keep uppermost in his mind the feelings and the sensitivities of the living, of the mourners who are seated before him, and must say nothing that will add to their grief.

Purchase of a Burial Place

23:3-20

Then Abraham rose from beside his dead and spoke to the children of Heth.

Abraham spoke words of comfort and consolation to the children of Heth who were bemoaning the death of Sarah. While Sarah was alive, the inhabitants of the area prospered in all their endeavors but once she died all beauty vanished and they became confused and uncertain. Therefore, they bewailed and bemoaned her passing. It was Abraham who had to console them, saying, "My children do not grieve.

This is the way of the world for the righteous as well as the wicked" (Midrash HaGadol).

It often happens at a funeral that people who are little more than casual acquaintances or distant relatives break out in loud, uncontrollable weeping, with the bereaved family having to comfort and console *them*. People attending a funeral or paying a Shivah visit should understand that it is their function to comfort the mourners and that loud and conspicuous expressions of grief on their part are in poor taste and often a sign of insincerity.

Although he loved Sarah deeply, Abraham did not fall to pieces when she died because he understood that "This is the way of the world for the righteous as well as the wicked." It is only natural to grieve at the passing of a loved one but it is also important to remember that "Man is born to die" and that the death of a loved one must not mean the end of a meaningful life for those who survive.

Abraham requests of the Children of Heth a burial place for Sarah. In speaking to them, he declares, *"I am a stranger and a sojourner with you."*

> Not only Abraham, but Moses, David and other great men referred to themselves as strangers. From this one can see how beloved is the stranger (Mechilta, Mishpatim 18).

The Jew has always had a special feeling for the stranger and a sensitivity to his needs because of his own experiences as a stranger, experiences which he never sought to hide or deny. The stranger should not be just the object of compassion but of love. "You shall love the stranger," declares the Torah (Deut. 10:19).

> From the fact that Abraham does not hesitate to refer to himself as *a stranger and a sojourner* we can see his humility, a trait which is one of the three distinguishing characteristics of the disciples of Abraham to this day (Avot d'Rabbi Nathan 44).

> One can learn a great deal about the character of Abraham from this incident. God had promised that

189

the entire land would belong to him and to his descendants forever and yet he could not find a burial place for Sarah without purchasing it from the children of Heth. Nevertheless, he did not complain against God or question God's actions. Even more, when he spoke to the children of Heth, he did so in all humility, referring to himself as *a stranger and a sojourner*. Therefore, God said to him, "Abraham, you have humbled yourself. Be assured that I will make you a lord and a prince over them" (Midrash HaGadol).

It is the man who is truly humble and who does not seek to lord it over others, who is most worthy of a position of respect and leadership. Honor comes not to him who runs after it but to the man who has earned it. Moses, David and other great leaders were selected precisely because they had shown themselves to be truly humble human beings, considerate of the feelings and the needs of all God's creatures, even dumb animals. Although Abraham was humble in his own eyes, the Children of Heth, in responding to him, call him a *mighty prince among us*.

Ephron, the owner of the property Abraham sought to purchase, at first declared, *"I give you the field and I give you the cave that is in it."* Yet in the end he exacted an exorbitant sum of *400 shekels of silver at the going merchant rate*.

This well illustrates the truth that the wicked promise much but do nothing at all, in contrast to the righteous who promise little but do much (Baba Metzia 87a).

The wicked person who has no intention of keeping his word does not hesitate to make all sorts of extravagant promises to entice and mislead his victim. The person who really intends to do something for others does not find it necessary to boast of what he will do. His actions speak eloquently for him (cf. on 18:7).

In responding to Ephron's original offer to give him the field for nothing, Abraham declares, *"I will give (Na'ta'ti) the price of the field."*

The verb *Na'ta'ti* is in the past tense. Thus the literal meaning of the words of Abraham is, "I gave the price of the field," to indicate that the word of a righteous person is equivalent to the act having already been done (Lekach Tov).

A man's word should be his bond. He must so conduct himself as to eliminate any shadow of doubt as to whether he will keep his word.

Once Abraham had made up his own mind that he was ready to pay for the field, he felt he no longer in good conscience could accept it for nothing (Sechel Tov).

Once an ethically sensitive person has decided to do something, even though the promise has not yet crossed his lips, he considers it a solemn obligation to fulfill what he intended. A pledge in one's own heart and mind is a valid pledge that should be kept even though it be unknown to anyone else.

Then Abraham buried his wife Sarah in the cave of the field of Machpelah, facing Mamre—now Hebron—in the land of Canaan. Thus the field with its cave passed from the children of Heth to Abraham as a burial site.

In the account of the purchase of the Cave of Machpelah and elsewhere, the phrase *Children of Heth* is to be found a total of ten times. How much ink has been spilled and how many quills have been broken in the writing! Why this seemingly unnecessary repetition? The ten times *Children of Heth* is mentioned correspond to the Ten Commandments, thus teaching that if one assists a righteous man in a purchase it is as though he fulfilled the Ten Commandments (Genesis Rabbah).

The proper conduct of business dealings is equated by Jewish tradition with the fulfillment of the entire Torah.

Honesty in business and the clear stipulation of all terms of purchase, so that there can be no possibility of fraud or misrepresentation, are solemn religious obligations.

> Why was it called the Cave of Machpelah? Machpelah means "double" and the cave was so called because it consisted of two stories or because various couples were to be buried there e.g. Adam and Eve, Abraham and Sarah, Isaac and Rebecca, Jacob and Leah (Pirkei d'Rabbi Eliezer).

The Cave of Machpelah is one of Judaism's most sacred places, second in sanctity only to the Western Wall. In it are buried all three patriarchs and three of the four matriarchs of the Jewish people. Despite this fact, until June, 1967 it was totally inaccessible to Jews. The world, which is so sensitive about Christian and Moslem Holy Places in Israel and so insistent upon free access for all, said not a word when Jordan barred Jews from the Cave of Machpelah in Hebron, the Western Wall in the Old City of Jerusalem, the Tomb of Rachel in Bethlehem and other places sacred to Judaism. Certainly, it is inconceivable that ever again a situation should be permitted to arise where Jews would be prevented from worshipping at their most sacred sites.

> The Cave of Machpelah was paid for by Abraham in full measure so that the nations of the world might never be able to accuse Israel of possessing it illegally (Genesis Rabbah).

No one can legitimately dispute the right of Israel to maintain control of the Cave of Machpelah. Since the days of Abraham, the title of the Jewish people to its most sacred burial ground has been clear. To emphasize the legality of Israel's claim, the Sages declare that the field and the cave passed to *Abraham as his possession* "through money, through deed, through witnesses and through the rights conferred by possession." By whatever yard-stick one chooses to measure legal rights the Jewish claim is unassailable.

CHAPTER 14

Abraham's Old Age

24:1

Abraham was now old, advanced in years, and the Lord had blessed Abraham in all things.

Why was Abraham privileged to live a long life? It was because all his life he pursued righteousness and loving-kindness; righteousness towards the living and loving-kindness towards the dead (Lekach Tov).

The Sages regarded long life as a mark of God's favor resulting from a life of righteousness. Rabbi Nechemiah ben HaKanah was asked by his disciples, "What is the reason for your longevity?" He replied, "I never gained honor for myself through the disgrace of my neighbor, I never harbored resentment against my neighbor and I was generous with my money" (Megillah 28a). Although, unfortunately, righteousness does not always result in long life for the *individual*, history proves that it does insure long life for society and for a people.

Abraham was privileged to enjoy long life because he performed the *mitzvah* of lovingly tending to all the details of the burial of Sarah. If Abraham was granted longevity for busying himself with the burial of a relative, how much more so is it with the one who busies himself with the burial of one who dies leaving no one to attend to his burial (Avot d'Rabbi Nathan).

It is a religious duty of the highest obligation to tend to the burial of a *met mitzvah*, one who dies without leaving relatives to attend his burial. In fact, Judaism regards paying the proper last respects to every deceased individual as being of utmost importance. Our Sages refer to it as *Chesed Shel Emet,* an act of true loving-kindness, because it is performed without any possibility of reward. They insisted that a man must interrupt even the study of Torah to assist in the preparations for burial and declared that one who sees a funeral procession and does not accompany the dead deserves to be banished from the community.

> Until Abraham, old age did not mark a person; people would mistake Isaac for his father Abraham and Abraham for Isaac because they looked exactly alike. Abraham prayed and he began to look his age (Baba Metzia 87a).

Abraham had no desire to try to look as young as his son. In our day, people go to ridiculous lengths to hide their age and to appear much younger than they are. They compete (unsuccessfully) with their children in dress and conduct in a futile attempt to roll back the years. They would be much happier if only they could learn to grow old gracefully. There is no disgrace in growing old. On the contrary, "the hoary head is a crown of glory" (Proverbs 16:31).

> The statement *Abraham was now old* follows immediately upon the burial of Sarah because when Sarah died, old age overtook Abraham (Tanchuma).

Husband and wife can grow old together, never noticing the passage of the years, enjoying one another's companionship and savouring life to its fullest. When one's spouse passes away, however, then old age is really felt and life can become a nightmare. It is loneliness that makes old age so unbearable for many. As the Sages put it, "A man who has no wife lives without joy, without blessing and without goodness" (Yevamot 62b).

> *Abraham was now old* in that he had acquired wisdom (Lekach Tov).

There are some who grow old without ever acquiring wisdom but the wisdom that comes from experience can be

194

acquired only by those who have lived many years. "As for scholars, the older they grow, the more wisdom they acquire, as it is said, 'With aged men is wisdom and in length of days understanding' (Job 12:12) ; but the ignorant as they grow older they become more foolish" (Shabbat 152a).

There are those who appear old although not advanced in years, while there are those who although advanced in years do not have the dignified appearance of old age. Abraham, however, *was now old, advanced in years,* meaning that his appearance corresponded to his age and his age to his appearance (Genesis Rabbah).

No one wants to look old and gray prematurely. On the other hand, dignity and beauty can accompany old age. It is a great blessing when, like Abraham, one is able to grow old gracefully and naturally.

Abraham was a source of blessing to all, as it says, *"All the families of the earth shall bless themselves by you"* (12:3). But who blessed Abraham? The Holy One Blessed Be He, for it says, *And the Lord had blessed Abraham in all things.* Similarly, Moses was the banner of Israel but who was Moses' banner? The Lord; David was the shepherd of Israel but who was David's shepherd? The Lord; Jerusalem is the light of the world but who is the light of Jerusalem? The Lord (Genesis Rabbah).

Although one should not perform a good deed out of expectation of receiving a reward, God does, in some way, reward those who exert themselves on behalf of others. Abraham may not have been rewarded by those whom he assisted but God Himself saw his actions and rewarded him for them. "Give to the world the best you have and the best will come back to you" (Mary Ainge DeVere).

What is meant by *in all things?* There is a dispute among the Sages on this point. Rabbi Judah maintained that it means that he was blessed in that he had a daughter, while Rabbi Meir held that he was

195

blessed in that he did not have a daughter (Baba Batra 16b).

Rabbi Judah insists that Abraham must have had a daughter, although she is not mentioned in the Torah, because otherwise his life would not have been completely blessed and it could not have been said of him, *The Lord had blessed Abraham in all things.* This indicates that daughters, contrary to the popular notion, were indeed regarded as a blessing. A daughter, even more so than a son, is a source of great joy and pleasure to her parents when she is young, and a great comfort to them when they are old. The contrary opinion of Rabbi Meir, that Abraham was blessed in that he did not have a daughter, simply reflects the fact that parents tend to worry about the moral development of a daughter more than of a son. "Through anxiety on her account, a parent cannot sleep at night; as a child lest she be seduced, as an adolescent lest she be immoral, as a mature woman lest she be not married, and if she marries lest she not have children" (Sanhedrin 100b). While parents do tend to worry more about their young daughters than about their sons, undoubtedly, most would agree with Rabbi Judah that the worry is far outweighed by the joy and pleasure that a daughter brings to a family and that truly a man is not blessed *in all things* until he is blessed with a daughter.

> *The Lord had blessed Abraham in all things* in that He blessed him in these three ways; He made him master over his evil inclination, during his lifetime his son Ishmael repented, and his treasure-house never lacked anything (Genesis Rabbah).

We tend to judge a man's blessings by his material success. Material success, however, was only one aspect of Abraham's blessing. The first aspect was his ability to control his impulses and master his evil inclinations. This is not a small matter. "Who is mighty?" ask the Sages. "He who is able to subdue his evil impulse" (Avot 4:1). This ability to control oneself is indeed a great blessing because if one is a slave to his impulses, appetites and passions,

196

then he is a slave indeed; cursed rather than blessed by God. Secondly, a man cannot be considered blessed and fortunate if his children have gone astray and are a source of unhappiness to him. Abraham's son, Ishmael, must have repented and reformed, say our Sages, or otherwise it could not have been said of Abraham that *the Lord had blessed him in all things.* Worldly possessions can be considered a blessing only when accompanied by mastery of oneself and by God-fearing children.

Eliezer's Mission

24:2-9

And Abraham said to the senior servant of his household who had charge of all that he owned, "Put your hand under my thigh and I will make you swear by the Lord, the God of heaven and the God of the earth, that you will not take a wife for my son from the daughters of the Canaanites among whom I dwell."

Abraham, by referring to the Lord as *the God of heaven and the God of the earth,* was affirming, "Before I made Him known to His creatures He was the *God of heaven* but since I made Him known to His creatures He is also *the God of the earth"* (Genesis Rabbah).

Not only does Man need God, God needs Man. God needs righteous men and women who will make Him known upon earth; who will create a respect for religion by demonstrating that religion has made them better, more ethical human beings. It is our sacred obligation to continue the task begun by Abraham, to so live as to make God not only the *God of heaven* but *the God of the earth,* as well.

What is the significance of the words *who had charge of all that he owned?* It means that he gave Eliezer control over all that he possessed and said to him, "Even if you must spend all that I have, see to it that my son not marry a daughter of the Canaanites" (Tanchuma, Buber, Va'yetze 3).

Abraham's fear lest his son marry a Canaanite girl is one that Jewish parents can sympathize and identify with. Intermarriage is on the increase and almost all Jewish parents, even those not otherwise concerned about Judaism and the Jewish heritage, are concerned and apprehensive lest their children marry out of the faith. Jewish opposition to intermarriage does not stem from bigotry or intolerance, as is frequently alleged by young people today. It is based upon the recognition that any intermarriage severs the links that have bound one generation to the next throughout the ages; it means the loss of a soul to Judaism and the Jewish people. Rampant intermarriage can well sound the death-knell of our faith. We are a small people and every defection from the Jewish fold is serious indeed. "When one marries out of the faith, causing himself and his offspring to leave the household of Israel, he is betraying the purpose and meaning of Jewish existence. He is turning his back on an embattled and persecuted people which has stubbornly and courageously maintained itself against the extraordinary forces which have throughout history sought to destroy it" (Jewish Tract Series: *Intermarriage*, p. 14).

Unlike many Jewish parents today who share his fear, however, Abraham did not leave the matter to chance. He spared no expense or effort to insure that his son would not marry a Canaanite girl. Parents today must be willing to do likewise. Although parents can no longer hope to choose their child's mate, wise parents can still guide their children so that they make the proper choice. When a child falls in love with a non-Jew, it is usually too late for parents to register effective opposition. Parents must begin proper religious training while the child is yet young so that upon growing up, he or she will feel an obligation and responsibility to seek only a Jewish mate. Parents can influence the eventual choice of a mate by their attitude towards seemingly harmless interdating, by their advice about the type of college the child should attend, by their own choice of a community in which to reside and in countless other ways, if only they are willing to invest the time and effort.

Abraham instructs his servant, *"Go to the land of my birth and get a wife for my son Isaac."*

> But were they not idol worshippers also? However, Abraham said, "Since I am going to have to convert someone, it is better to convert a member of my own family, for they should come first. Not only that, but they are more likely to reform." From this we can learn that a man should be most concerned about those who are closest to him and, if he is able, he should be of assistance to them. Thus it is said, "Hide not thyself from thine own flesh" (Isaiah 58:7)—(Midrash HaGadol).

Although we have an obligation to all mankind, our first responsibility is to our own families. Not only that, but we are much more likely to succeed in influencing for good those who are nearest to us than in influencing those who are strangers to us. The story is told of a man who set out to reform the world but failed miserably. Upon realizing that he had failed, he decided to concentrate on reforming his community. Failing there as well, he came to the conclusion that he had best concentrate on himself and the members of his family and, thereby, he could most effectively influence the world.

Abraham failed in his mission to convert the idolators among whom he lived but his life was a shining success and his influence is still felt in the world because he succeeded in winning to his ideals and way of life his own son, Isaac, and his daughter-in-law, Rebecca. Unwise indeed are those who expend so much effort trying to influence others that they have no time to mold the lives of their own children and grandchildren.

> The fact that Abraham was so anxious for Isaac to marry one of his own illustrates the proverb, "Even if the wheat of your own locality is not of the

199

best quality, sow with it, nevertheless" (Genesis Rabbah).

Young Jews contemplating intermarriage will sometimes argue that they have found qualities of mind and character in the prospective non-Jewish mate that they have been unable to find in a Jewish partner. Although it may be true that the prospective mate is an unusually fine person, there are questions to be considered in addition to that of loyalty to one's faith and people. Marriage is always a risky proposition but when husband and wife come from completely different religious backgrounds, the problems are compounded and the chances of failure are much greater.

In his book *If You Marry Outside Your Faith*, Bishop James Pike sums up the results of a study concerning broken marriages among mixed couples of Catholic and Protestant origin. "In short, there was in the case of mixed marriages two and one quarter (2¼) times as much separation and divorce as in the families where there was religious homogeneity." In the case of intermarriage between a Jew and a non-Jew, where the differences of background and outlook are even more pronounced, it is likely that the figure would be still greater. A concern generally overlooked until it is too late, is the effect such differences have upon the child of an intermarriage, who is likely to grow up confused and rootless, not knowing where he belongs, an outcast in the culture of both his parents.

CHAPTER 15

Abraham Remarries

25:1-6

After the marriage of his son, Isaac, to Rebecca, *Abraham took another wife whose name was Keturah.*

If you have had children in your youth, take a wife in old age. From whom do you learn this? From Abraham who had children in his younger years, yet took a wife in his old age and had children (Genesis Rabbah).

A widow or widower need not feel guilty of disloyalty to a beloved first spouse by contemplating remarriage. A desire to remarry and enjoy the blessings of companionship in one's old age is not an insult to the departed but a tribute to the happiness of married life, and a recognition of the blessings that only matrimony can bring.

Isaac, after his own marriage to Rebecca, said, "Is it right that I have taken a wife and my father should remain without a wife?" What did Isaac do? He went and found a wife for his father (Tanchuma).

Not only did Isaac not oppose his father's remarriage, he actively encouraged it and helped to arrange it. The fact that his own inheritance might be somewhat diminished thereby did not concern him in the least. Sometimes, children oppose a parent's remarriage for either sentimental reasons or financial considerations or both. They could well learn from Isaac's attitude towards Abraham's remarrying, that they have no right to deny a parent some measure of happiness in his remaining years.

Abraham did not remarry until he had arranged for the marriage of his son, Isaac. From this you can learn that if a man's wife passes away and he has grownup children, he should first marry off his children and only then take a wife himself (Genesis Rabbah).

A parent's first responsibility is to his children. He must not neglect their needs while seeking his own personal fulfillment. Only after having properly provided for the welfare and happiness of his children, does a parent have the right to provide for his own happiness through remarriage. Of course, since children need the loving care of both a mother and a father, the very act of remarriage can become a means of meeting parental responsibilities towards one's children.

We are told that *Abraham took another wife* immediately after we are told that *Isaac took Rebekah as his wife. Isaac loved her and thus found comfort after his mother's death.* From this juxtaposition we learn the truth of the proverb, "Sixty pangs come upon a man who hears his neighbor eating and is unable to eat himself" (Baba Kamma 92b).

While his son Isaac was unmarried and immersed in sorrow as he was, it was easier for Abraham to bear the pain of Sarah's passing. After Isaac found comfort and companionship in marriage, however, Abraham felt his loss more keenly than before. There is truth in the Hebrew saying, "The suffering of the multitude is a partial consolation." It is easier to reconcile oneself to sorrow and suffering when others are undergoing the same experience. When one is alone in his suffering, however, while others are enjoying life to its fullest, the pain becomes almost unbearable and such a person should not be criticized for trying to experience a small measure of the happiness that others possess.

Undoubtedly, the growing discontent of underprivileged minority groups in our country today can be traced, at least in part, to the fact that through television and other communications media they have become increasingly aware of the material blessings enjoyed by other segments of the population. This increased awareness of the prosperity of others has made them less willing to accept passively their own poverty.

Rabbi Judah maintains that Keturah was Hagar whom Abraham had remarried. Why then was she called Keturah? The name Keturah implies that she bound together (*Kitrah*) in herself commandments and good deeds (Genesis Rabbah).

Although Hagar was the mother of Ishmael, whose descendants were the arch-enemies of Israel, the Sages refused to blacken her name in order to discredit her progeny. She is depicted as pious and noble and as having maintained the highest standards of morality after having been banished by Abraham on account of the wickedness of her son, Ishmael. Here we have a wonderful example of the tolerance and broad-mindedness of our Sages who rejected the concept of "guilt by association" and heaped praise upon Hagar despite her kinship with an enemy of the Jewish people.

Others maintain that Keturah was not Hagar but Abraham's third wife and point out that each of his three wives was descended from a different son of Noah; Sarah being a descendant of Shem, Hagar of Ham and Keturah of Japhet (Yalkut Shim'oni, Job 904).

The descendants of the three sons of Noah represent, of course, the various races and nationalities of mankind and the Sages are here emphasizing that our Father Abraham bore no prejudice against any race or nationality. Judaism is not a matter of race or national origin. Anyone who sincerely adopts the way of life represented by Judaism can become a Jew.

Keturah bore Abraham many children but *Abraham willed all that he owned to Isaac*.

Rabbi Judah maintains that this refers to the birthright. Rabbi Nehemiah maintains that it refers to the ability to confer blessing (cf. 12:2). The Rabbis maintain that it refers to the right of burial in the Cave of Machpelah and a will giving Isaac all his possessions (Genesis Rabbah).

Although material possessions formed part of his inheritance, Isaac's inheritance from his father must be understood primarily in spiritual terms. That the privileges of the birthright were mainly spiritual and not material can be seen from the fact that *Esau despised his birthright* (25:34), which he certainly would not have done had it carried with it material advantages. As to the ability to confer blessing, it was at the very beginning of his spiritual career that Abraham had been told by the Almighty, *"You shall be a blessing."* This injunction to be a source of blessing to all mankind was transmitted by Abraham to Isaac alone and has been amply fulfilled by the descendants of Isaac throughout the generations.

Abraham conceived of his bequest to his beloved son and successor in spiritual and ethical terms and the example of the first Jew has been emulated by subsequent generations. There is an entire literature of Jewish Ethical Wills in which parents, ignoring their material possessions as being unimportant, seek to impart their spiritual values and ideals to their children. The ethical will of Judah Ibn Tibbon who lived in Spain in the 12th century is a good example. In his will he admonishes his son "to behave in a friendly spirit toward all, to gain a good name, to revere God and perform His commandments."

But to Abraham's sons by concubines, Abraham gave gifts while he was still living; and he sent them away from his son Isaac eastward, to the land of the East.

The descendants of Ishmael and the descendants of Keturah came before Alexander the Great to dispute with Israel, claiming that the Land of Israel should be shared jointly by all the descendants of Abraham. Geviah ben Pesisa countered their argument, however. "If you seek to prove your point from the Torah, I can refute your claim from the

Torah. It is written, *Abraham willed all that he owned to Isaac but to Abraham's sons by concubines Abraham gave gifts while he was still living; and he sent them away.* If a father banished his sons during his lifetime and sent them away, can they possibly have any claim whatsoever?" (Sanhedrin 91a).

All sorts of spurious arguments are adduced to challenge the validity of the Jewish claim to the Land of Israel. The record, however, is clear. Whether on religious, historical or practical grounds, the Jewish claim to the Land of Israel is unchallengeable, and every argument brought by our enemies cannot withstand the light of logic and reason.

He sent them away from his son Isaac eastward, to the land of the East. Said Abraham to them, "My son, Isaac, is a youngster and any nation that will subjugate him or his descendants will be driven into *Gehinnom.* Therefore, go and settle in the East. As long as the descendants of Isaac are enslaved among the nations, stay in your place but when you hear that they are dwelling in safety and tranquility come and minister to them in order that you may merit the Shofar of the Messiah" (Midrash HaGadol).

As long as the Jewish people were in exile, subjugated and oppressed in Europe and elsewhere, the descendants of Ishmael did remain in their places in the East, exhibiting no particular affinity for, or attachment to, Palestine and certainly doing nothing to build the land. Only a relative handful of Arabs lived in Palestine prior to the return of the Jews. Arab interest in Palestine was aroused only when Jews returned to the Land and sought to rebuild it in peace. Had the Arabs proferred the hand of friendship to the returning exiles, they would have indeed merited the Shofar of the Messiah in that they would have benefitted immeasurably from their contact with the descendants of Isaac. Instead, they came with violence and bloodshed, thus denying to their downtrodden masses the benefits that could have been theirs and that could have improved their lot to a point which would have been a foretaste of the Messianic Era.

Death of Abraham

25:7-8

And these are the days of the years of Abraham's life which he lived, a hundred threescore and fifteen years.

What is the significance of the seeming redundancy, *which he lived?* It indicates that he really lived all the days of his life (Midrash HaGadol).

Abraham knew how to live every day of his life, an art that is increasingly rare in our day. We have succeeded in adding years to man's life. Now we face an even greater challenge—adding life to these years. It has been correctly observed that it is not how old you are that is really significant, but how you are old.

Abraham lived to the age of 175 while Isaac lived to the age of 180. Why did he live five years less than his son? God withheld five years from the life of Abraham because his grandson Esau committed the outrageous sins of rape and murder. Said God, "I promised Abraham, *'you shall go to your fathers in peace; you shall be buried at a ripe old age'* (15:15). What kind of a good and peaceful old age would it be if he should see his grandson guilty of idolatry, immorality and murder? It would be better for him to depart this world in peace" (Genesis Rabbah, Toldot 63).

There is nothing that renders an aged parent or grandparent more unhappy than seeing a child or grandchild go astray. It was truly a manifestation of God's love for Abraham that he did not live to experience the anguish and heartache that Esau's actions would have caused him.

The death of a loved one is always an occasion for sorrow but it should not lead us to question the wisdom and goodness of God. The truly pious individual realizes that he cannot fathom the ways of God or understand His purposes but he is convinced that there is a reason, though it be known only to God. "All that God does, He does for the best," is the attitude that the pious Jew adopts and maintains, no matter what inexplicable tragedy befalls him.

And Abraham breathed his last, dying at a good, ripe age, old and contented; and he was gathered to his kin.

On the day that Abraham our Father departed from this world, the leaders of the nations of the world stood in line and exclaimed, "Woe unto the world for it has lost its leader; woe unto the ship for it has lost its captain" (Baba Batra 91b).

The death of Abraham was a grievous loss not only for his own family and people but for all mankind. Abraham had been a source of blessing to all, Jew and non-Jew alike. Although during his lifetime his efforts were not always appreciated and his ideals were often mocked and scorned, after he was gone the leaders of the nations of the world came to realize how important his life had been for their own well-being and welfare. Indeed, from that day until this, the life of Abraham and the ideals he proclaimed have served as a constant source of inspiration and guidance to all those who have sought to live as decent, upright men and women. Abraham *our* Father is truly the *spiritual* father of every God-fearing human being.

INDEX

210

211

SIDRA INDEX

FESTIVALS AND SPECIAL SABBATHS